Edgar Cayce on the Reincarnation of Biblical Characters

Edgar Cayce on the Reincarnation of Biblical Characters

by Kevin J. Todeschi

A.R.E. Press • Virginia Beach • Virginia

1st Printing, November 1999

Printed in the U.S.A.

A.R.E. Press
215 67th Street
Virginia Beach, VA 23451-2061

Todeschi, Kevin J.
Edgar Cayce on the reincarnation of biblical characters / by Kevin J. Todeschi.
p. cm.
ISBN 0-87604-462-3 (pbk)
1. Cayce, Edgar, 1877-1945. Edgar Cayce Readings. 2. Reincarnation Biography. 3. Bible—Biography—Miscellanea. I. Title.
BL519.T62 1999
133.9'01'35—dc21 99-36227

Cover design by Lightbourne

Contents

INTRODUCTION

Of the more than 14,000 readings given by Edgar Cayce over a forty-three-year period, approximately 2,000 deal with the subject of reincarnation. From Cayce's perspective, each of us goes through a series of lifetimes for the express purpose of soul growth and development. In that process, the soul is given opportunities and experiences which will best enable the individual to fulfill the purpose for which she or he incarnated. In the language of the readings, the individual is given whatever conditions are needed "to meet the needs of that to make the entity at an at oneness with the Creative Energy." (254-32)

The readings on reincarnation were given to individuals in order to help them understand soul strengths and weaknesses, as well as their own potentials and challenges. As Cayce entered his trance state, he was given a specific suggestion that enabled him to access the necessary information for a "life reading," which dealt with the soul's history. That suggestion was as follows:

> You will have before you the life existence in the earth plane (giving name, date, where) and the earthly existence of this entity in that of (giving

> name and place of the earthly sojourn) and you will give a biographical life of the entity in that day and plane of earthly existence, from entrance and how into the earth's plane and the entity's departure, giving the development or retarding points in such an existence. 254-22

Cayce's response to that suggestion would provide the individual with a historical timeline of her or his incarnations, lessons learned, as well as any faults or patterns that had been acquired and needed to be overcome in the present.

Critics of reincarnation often point out that many individuals believe that they were a Cleopatra or a George Washington or some famous personage from the annals of history. Whatever happened to all of the common people? Where are all the farmers, the housewives, the peasants, the prisoners, or the uneducated masses that made up the bulk of history's population? Although the Cayce readings did give a number of famous identities from the past, the majority of the life readings are filled with names of individuals who were everyday people. In fact, of the more than 10,000 names given in past-life readings, less than two percent are identifiable as "famous." Of that number, approximately half are characters from the Bible.

Throughout his life, the Bible played an extremely important role for Edgar Cayce. By the time he was a teenager, he had managed to read it through once for every year of his life—a practice he maintained until his death. Raised a devout Christian, he was a lifelong Sunday school teacher, the Bible becoming the basis for his life and teachings. However, the material in Cayce's readings is deeply ecumenical. Edgar Cayce urged individuals to pursue their own religious preferences, stating that "oneness" should be the undergirding principle of any spiritual journey. From his perspective, what was most important in a person's life was one's application of spiritual principles.

Regardless of an individual's religious preference, however, Cayce believed that the Bible was a handbook for self-understanding. From Genesis to Revelation it portrayed the story of each soul's unfolding experiences in the earth. The readings state that we are spiritual beings undergoing a physical experience, and the Bible portrays the overall development in our consciousness in this dimension. For that reason, the early stories in the Old Testament are not necessarily to be understood as acceptable behavior today. For example, when Lot's two daughters get their father drunk in order to sleep with him and conceive to insure the continuation of his ancestral line, it is not an endorsement of incest but rather a portrayal of a time in our own consciousness when we believed physical heredity superior to our spiritual source. Rather than being a book that simply had meaning for our ancestors, Cayce stated that the Bible provided important insights even in the present:

> For, it tells of God, of your home, of His dealings with His peoples in many environs, in many lands. Read it to be wise. Study it to understand. *Live* it to know that the Christ walks through same with thee.
>
> 262-60

In addition to specific Bible stories, frequently the readings encouraged people to read John 14-17 and Deuteronomy 30, where they could find a *personal* message, applicable in their daily lives.

Cayce also believed that the Bible had a threefold interpretation. Most stories possessed a physical, a psychological, and a spiritual meaning. The characters in the Bible actually lived as real people. In addition to being real people, many of the characters symbolized a psychological state of consciousness (for example, Abraham symbolizes faith; Job symbolizes patience), and each story contained an archetypal meaning which was just as true and applicable today. For example, the story of Noah and the Flood is an archetype of being overwhelmed by personal experience and being transformed to a higher state of awareness in the process. The story of the Prodigal Son is an archetype of the soul's journey (we were with God in the beginning, embarked on a journey, and are in the process of returning to Him with a greater degree of awareness); and so on.

In all, the Bible contains approximately 3,000 characters—a number of whom possess the very same name. When an individual received a life reading and was told that he or she had been a biblical character from the past, it is sometimes necessary to isolate to whom Cayce is referring. For example, the Old Testament refers to three individuals with the name Abimelech: one known by Abraham, another who was a brutal ruler and served as one of the judges of Israel, and the third who was the Philistine king of Gath known to David. The individual who was told by Edgar Cayce that he had been Abimelech was told "in Abraham's day" (699-1), clearly identifying the specific identity.

With the premise that we might somehow glimpse aspects of the continuity of life by reviewing the soul histories of others, this volume presents an overview of those readings that identified the individual as having been a character from the Bible. It does not include case histories for those who were not directly or indirectly referred to in Scripture, nor does it include identities for those who were related to or simply associated with a biblical character; only those individuals who were given biblical identities themselves have been included.

Biblical Characters Mentioned

Abatha
Exodus 2:1-10
Case 5373

According to the Book of Exodus, while the children of Israel were slaves in the land of Egypt there came a time when Pharaoh feared that the number of Hebrew men and boys had grown too vast. Fearing a possible slave uprising, Pharaoh ordered that all male children born to the Hebrews were to be killed. One Hebrew woman managed to hide her son for three months before deciding to set him adrift on the river in a cask made of bulrushes, in the hopes that he might find safety. The boy's sister, Miriam, watched the floating cask to see what would happen to him. (See also "Miriam.") Once adrift, the daughter of Pharaoh spotted the small craft while she was bathing. She sent her maid to fetch the basket and when they saw that the basket contained a child, Pharaoh's daughter decided to call the child "Moses" because he had been drawn from the river. Although not named specifically in the Bible, Edgar Cayce stated that the young maid who had pulled the baby Moses from the river was called Abatha.

In 1944, a forty-eight-year-old woman seeking vocational advice was told that she possessed the talents of both a confidant and a counselor. Apparently, people were drawn to her and felt at ease telling her their problems. Her reading informed her that she could excel in research, in the gathering of data or statistics, as a teacher or even as a secretary.

Her most notable past lives included a trek in the Old West, where she had acquired her love for nature; living in the Holy Land, where she had been one of the children whom Jesus blessed; and a life in Egypt as a maid to Pharaoh's daughter:

> Before that we find the entity was in the Egyptian land when there were those beginnings of the preparation for the coming of the lawgiver. The entity was among those of the maids to the princess of Egypt, and the individual who waded into the river to bring the little ark or bassinet ashore with the babe in same . . . The name then was Abatha.
>
> 5373-1

Her reading went on to promise her some vocational and relationship changes within a year. Although Edgar Cayce's secretary, Gladys Davis, asked the woman for an update in 1947, no follow-up reports are on file until 1950 when it was learned that [5373] was operated on for a brain tumor. The woman died within a couple of years of the operation.

Abimelech
Genesis 20, 21, 26
Case 699

When Abraham journeyed into Gerar with his wife, Sarah, he was afraid that other men would want to possess her and would slay him in order to have his wife. As a result, he told the people that Sarah was his sister. Upon seeing Sarah, Abimelech, the king, wanted her and decided to take her into his harem. However, God warned the king in a dream that she was already married to Abraham. Fearful of retribution, Abimelech immediately returned Sarah to her rightful husband. The two men eventually exchanged gifts and made a covenant of friendship. Years later, Abimelech would again be faced with an almost identical situation when Isaac, Abraham's son, tried to pass off his own wife, Rebekah, as his sister. This time, however, Abimelech quickly saw through the ruse.

Immediately after coming in contact with the Cayce work, a thirty-four-year-old physicist reported that he had finally found that for which he had always been seeking. He obtained a physical reading for a friend, procured his own life reading, and was present for a number of readings, including one in which he asked about the possibility of helping to manage the Cayce work.

In his reading, Cayce told [699] that he possessed broad vision and the capacity to acquire position, power, responsibility, and money. However, Cayce also stated that [699] was not likely to follow through on his true potential unless he held to his goals. Quick to act in all things, he also maintained a deep interest in spirituality and the mysteries of life. Because of his experiences in a number of previous lives, he possessed an innate fear regarding what others might say about his activities. In his most recent past life he had served as an assistant to Robert Fulton in the development of a steam engine. Previously, in England, he had served as a captain in the Crusades but had gained a deep respect for the Islamic faith as well as a tolerance for other people. It was in Palestine that he eventually befriended Abraham:

> The entity then gained, even through those experiences and associations. Yet from those very activities there were brought those desires on the part of the entity, Abimelech, to bring to the knowledge

> of those who were as servants—or those whom the entity served in the capacity of the king of that land—that, "He that would be the greatest among all would be the servant of all." While the entity had much in its experience and through that sojourn, that in the material and the moral life in the present would be questioned, yet the purposes, the aims, the desires, the activities were rather as the growth throughout that sojourn. 699-1

In an earlier incarnation in Egypt, he had served as a doctor, utilizing the forces of nature in his healing modalities.

In the present, [699] was encouraged to apply himself in the field of electrical therapeutics. If he did so, the reading stated, he would eventually work wonders and discover how to help restore health through physical regeneration.

According to the notations on file, [699] eventually referred a number of individuals to Edgar Cayce for readings. He also wrote the Cayce Association a number times during the 1950s describing his thankfulness for having been exposed to the Cayce information. However, no follow-up vocational reports are on file. The final notation is from 1968 when [699] wrote Edgar's son, Hugh Lynn, and stated, "I am especially grateful for my life reading and the many visits I had with him [Edgar Cayce] in Washington."

Abner

I Samuel 14, 17, 20, 26; II Samuel 2-4; I Kings 2;
I Chronicles 26, 27
Case 1815

Saul was the first king of Israel. His cousin and the valiant captain of his army was Abner. A number of battles against the Philistines began to mobilize the people of Israel and strengthen Saul's rule. However, Saul soon befriended a young musician, David, who rose in popularity with the people. As a result, Saul became increasingly jealous of the fact that the people liked someone more than himself, and he swore to have David killed. It was Abner who was forced to follow through on many of Saul's insane demands to track down David. David was successful in always eluding Saul's armies. After Saul eventually committed suicide, David and Abner befriended one another, and Abner swore his own allegiance to David, the new king of Israel. Unfortunately, Joab, a ruthless soldier in David's army, had Abner ambushed and killed in revenge for an earlier battle between the two. The death brought much sadness and regret to King David.

In 1939, a woman requested a reading for herself for a physical problem and a life reading for her fifteen-year-old son in order to help him with his education and development. Trained in musical composition, the boy liked the piano and wondered about being a music teacher. His mother, however, was concerned about his material success and felt that music would not help him to be as "self-supporting" as she desired him to be.

In tracing the boy's past lives, Cayce stated that [1815]'s love for music was due, in part, to a time during the Crusades when he was associated with those in command and often led the troops in the song of battle, inspiring them to work together for victory. That ability in the present would enable him to bring large groups of people together. Previously, at the time of the birth of Jesus, the boy had been one of the shepherds upon the hillsides of Bethlehem who had been stunned to hear the angels sing, "Glory to God in the highest—peace on earth and good will to all." During that same incarnation he had developed his musical abilities, specifically on the harp and reed instruments. Innately, [1815] possessed the ability to use music to move people into a closer relationship with their Creator. The boy's life as Abner had brought growth as well as retrogression:

> Before that we find the entity was among those who were close to the king who was proclaimed after Saul—or a friend of, a companion of David; and raised to one in power—yet the experience became both an advancement as well as a retardment.
>
> For the entity allowed self, and the power of self, to become as the greater influence.
>
> The name then was Abner. 1815-1

Cayce stated that the boy's love for music was also traceable to a prior incarnation in Egypt when he had directed song and dance in the various temples.

During the course of the reading, the boy's mother was told that her son had a natural inclination for leadership and possessed the ability to sway great numbers of people. Wherever his life took him, he would not remain in the background but would be in the forefront. He was a natural leader and politician. The reading also stated that he was very susceptible to the opposite sex, could excel in a musical career or politics, and was extremely intuitive. Because his incarnations gave quite a variety of possible outlets in the present, Cayce stated that [1815] would be drawn to both material things and music, but that music could give him the greatest outlet for his talents.

After the reading, his mother wrote several times to thank Cayce for the information. The boy also wrote an article about his personal philosophy that was printed by the Association a short time later. It was in 1979, however, that Mr. [1815], who had become a nationally known stock market analyst (sometimes labeled a "soothsayer" for his accuracy), submitted a complete follow-up report:

> I always knew who I was and where I was going from the very earliest age. Richly endowed by parents of opposite backgrounds, I got my great physical strength from my father and my artistic temperament from my mother. My father had little education, came from poverty and had to work very hard from an early age for everything he got. He gave me my drive, ambition, and the credo to always keep going and never give up. My mother gave me my great love of life, its total freedom, my deep love for music and books. Some of my earliest memories consisted of the two of us sitting out under the stars at night, my asking her at the age of four as to people living on other planets. She taught me to play piano when I was three. We had a very extensive library and I always had my nose in a book. As for the piano, I had a great talent for improvisation. It has never left me. That talent was extended to describe everything I do. I have always been the maverick, the iconoclast, the breaker of accepted images. Everything I touched led to new contributions of thought, new theories—always the pioneer.

In 1941, at the age of seventeen, [1815] published his first book. While attending Duke University he developed a keen interest in chemistry and economics. Although he married briefly in 1944, before being called to serve in World War II, the marriage was annulled after the war. During the war he also wrote a book on predicting the price of the stock market; the book went through a number of editions and became a big success. He also wrote other volumes on the market and investments and created a self-published newsletter in 1950 because of his knack for predicting market fluctuations. That newsletter would eventually include subscribers throughout the country.

His talents were in many directions: writing, public speaking, acting, music, mathematics, and statistical analysis. His success with the market and his investment strategies caused him to become so well known that Mike Wallace once interviewed him in an hourlong CBS television special. In a copy of his market letter in 1980, [1815] wrote about his early experience with Edgar Cayce and stated: "Everything in that life reading has been dramatically fulfilled."

Achlar
Matthew 2
Case 1908

According to the New Testament, Wise Men journeyed from the East following a star which they believed heralded the birth of the Christ child. King Herod had heard of them and summoned them to his court, requesting that once the child was discovered they tell him where the infant might be found. The Wise Men continued their journey to Bethlehem, found the babe, and offered gifts of gold, frankincense, and myrrh. Afterward, they were warned in a dream not to return to Herod; therefore, they traveled back to their country by another route. Although they were not specifically named in the Bible, Edgar Cayce gave two individuals life readings and stated that each had been one of the Wise Men: Achlar and Ashtueil. (See also "Ashtueil.")

A forty-nine-year-old science editor was told that his critical mind had become a fault as often as it was a virtue. He was encouraged to formulate and then live in accord with a spiritual ideal, being more loving in his interactions with others. Interested in things of a mystical nature, he was informed that he had been an astrologer, a counselor, and a sage during the time of Jesus:

> In those periods that preceded the advent of the Prince of Peace in the earth, we find the entity was among those of the land that would now be called the Persian—as a wise man, a counselor, a sage, that counseled with those peoples; using the mathematical activities of the ages old, as well as the teachings of the Persians from the days of Zend and Og and Uhjltd, bringing for those peoples a better interpretation of the astrological as well as the natural laws.
>
> Hence we find the entity was associated oft with those who looked for the day, the hour when that *great purpose,* that event, was to be in the earth a literal experience.
>
> Then we find the entity was among those of the fabled as well as real experience, seeking with the Wise Men that came from the East during those periods.
>
> In the present experience of the entity, then, we find that those oft told tales are accepted deep within because of the conviction and purpose such have produced and do produce in the hearts and the minds of individuals.
>
> We find this entity was the one who brought the incense to the child Jesus—in the name then Achlar. In the experience the entity gained, the entity manifested its love for its fellow man through those periods of activity in the search for the helpful influences, mentally, spiritually, materially; though the entity then lost sight oft of materiality.
>
> Thus the entity, in its application of and search for scientific purposes and reasons, should lean the

> more heavily upon the mental and spiritual phases of man's experience in the present.
>
> And, as in those days, give the more oft *hope* where that of dread as to the material things is overshadowing man in his search for God. 1908-1

Mr. [1908] had also had an incarnation in Ireland as a man of great physical prowess and strength. At that time, he had frequently had the opportunity to demonstrate his abilities. He had lived in Atlantis and had been one of those who had looked for safety lands to which the people could migrate, gaining a knowledge of the Yucatan, the Pyrenees, and Egypt. In the present, he was told to keep the same faith that had enabled him to find the child in Bethlehem. He could become of greatest service to humankind through his writing abilities.

File reports indicate that Mr. [1908] remained firmly committed to the Cayce work until his death in August 1953.

Achsah

Joshua 15:16-19; Judges 1:12-15; I Chronicles 2:49
Case 1294

Caleb was a scout to Moses and one of only two individuals from the original tribe allowed to enter the Promised Land. Caleb promised his daughter, Achsah, in marriage to whoever could conquer the city of Debir. Othniel defeated the city and claimed Achsah as his wife. Acshah also asked for and received from her father a dowry of land that included some springs of water, enabling her and her husband to begin a new life together.

A thirty-one-year-old Jewish woman was told that she had been associated with both her present husband and son in her life as Achsah. At the time, her husband had been a companion and her son, [1292], had been her father, Caleb. (See also "Caleb.")

> Before that we find the entity's experience that becomes the greater of its activities; when there were those journeyings from the land of Egypt to the land of promise.
>
> The entity then was the daughter of a leader, Caleb, that brought such a report of the land to all those travellers, those peoples of promise, those chosen that were to give to the world the basic principles for their moral and spiritual life.
>
> The entity was born in the wilderness, and was given in marriage when there was the conquering and the activity of the father's people in the taking and settling of the lands about the Holy City.
>
> Then in the name Achsah . . . 1294-1

Her reading informed her that she was both sensitive and practical and possessed a deep desire to live a spiritual life. Tolerant to the ideas of others, she was a true humanitarian. Extremely intelligent and skilled in creating a home life, [1294] was told that she would have the opportunity to influence both national and international activities, especially in the latter part of her life.

In addition to her incarnation as Achsah, she had lived during the early settling of western Pennsylvania, where she had learned love and tolerance and being of service to those who were in need. During a lifetime in France, she had learned to love life for its everyday experiences and for its relationships and associations with others. She had served as an emissary to other lands during an Egyptian incarnation and had learned to use her intuition to work with others. Throughout her incarnations she had excelled in tolerance and open-mindedness. Her reading also told her that she possessed skill as a writer that would show itself in her latter years.

According to the reports on file, [1294]'s husband died six months later because he had not followed advice he had been given in a physical reading. In 1952, she requested and received a copy of her son's life reading to which she responded: "Thank you so much for the copy of [1292]'s life reading. It is most interesting to me since he is now a young man and he also will enjoy following his life's reading as the years go by."

No additional reports are on file.

Ahijah

I Kings 11, 12, 14, 15; II Chronicles 9:29, 10:15
Case 4087

Ahijah was a prophet who lived during the time of Solomon and Jeroboam. Ahijah prophesied to Jeroboam that because Solomon had rejected God and instead turned to his love of power and taxes, the tribes of Israel would be divided. To illustrate his prophecy, Ahijah tore his coat into twelve pieces and gave ten to Jeroboam. Later, at Solomon's death, Jeroboam became the first king of the ten northern tribes.

Parents of a six-year-old boy came to Edgar Cayce for a reading in 1944 in part to discover why their son had undergone such "unusual psychical experiences" in his life. They sought advice on his religious and educational training.

Cayce told the parents that their child had been endowed with great possibilities as well as great problems that he needed to meet. On more than one occasion, the boy had been gifted with "second sight" and could see "visions of things to come, of things that are happening." In one incarnation the boy had been alive at the time of Jesus, when he had known Peter. The only other incarnation mentioned was when their son had been the prophet who had warned Jereboam of the division of the tribes of Israel. The parents were advised to read about that experience in Scripture.

His training was to focus on the things of the spirit, the things of the divine, rather than upon those things for the gratifying or satisfying of self. The boy's intuitive gifts could be used to help many, but only after a firm spiritual foundation had been established. Cayce promised that [4087] could be of great help to many. In terms of the boy's psychic experiences, the parents were also told, "Do not discourage, do not encourage the visions—until the first lessons are learned":

> Here the parents have a real, real obligation. They have a real, real opportunity. So live in self that thine own lives may be an example to this entity through its formative years. So teach, not let it be given to someone else—so teach, for it is thy responsibility, not the priest's, not a teacher's, *not* a minister's responsibility, but thine. Don't put it off. Don't neglect, or else ye will meet self again. 4087-1

Throughout the reading, Cayce reminded the parents of their important obligation in their son's upbringing and also encouraged them to give their child a love of spirituality and recommending specific biblical passages that would be useful in his training.

The only note on file states that [4087]'s parents went through a period of marital difficulties. No additional follow-up reports are available.

Andrew

Matthew 4:18-22, 10:1-4; Mark 1:16-21, 29; 3:14-19, 13:3-37; Luke 6:13-16; John 1:39-51, 6:1-15, 12:21-32; Acts 1:12-14

Case 341

Patron saint of Scotland, Andrew is best known for having been chosen as the first of Jesus' twelve apostles. The brother of Simon Peter and the son of John of Bethsaida, Andrew was a disciple of John the Baptist from whom he first heard about Jesus. A fisherman by trade, he brought Jesus to the attention of his brother, Simon Peter, and the two were told, "Follow me, and I will make you fishers of men." Andrew was also the individual who brought the young boy with the loaves and fishes to Jesus when the five thousand who had come to hear Jesus speak grew hungry. The loaves and the fishes provided the materials with which Jesus performed a miracle and fed the five thousand their fill. Tradition holds that Andrew was martyred in Greece.

In 1923, parents of a sixteen-year-old student obtained the first life reading for their son. They were told that their son had many talents and could excel as a writer, a historian, an orator, or one whose field of study would lie in the direction of things of a spiritual nature. Extremely intelligent, their son had past-life experiences as a monk, as a warrior during the Crusades, in ancient Egypt as a Pharaoh, and in Palestine as Andrew, one of the original disciples. Later readings would state that the lifetimes in Palestine and Egypt would hold the greatest influence in the boy's present experience.

Several years after his first life reading, [341] requested an additional reading to provide further information on his incarnation as Andrew. That reading stated, in part:

> This experience then, especially in that physical body known as Andrew, we find the entity then the

second brother in a family of four, and in the early childhood one willful in many ways, taking up the physical vocation of the parents and brother, and in the days when John [the Baptist] began to teach in the wilderness, the entity, the body (physical), Andrew, became first an adherent and a disciple of that teacher, and remained close as an aide, from first conviction, until the appearance of Jesus to become the disciple of the entity's master. When pointed out by John as the one that should be greater, and increase as he decreased, Andrew then followed the new leader into the wilderness, and was close with Him during the temptation, as is recorded by Matthew, and when the return to the seashore, sought out the brother [Peter], telling of those ideas, ideals, as were propounded by Him who had been pointed out, and became the close disciple then of the Teacher and Master, following close throughout the whole physical career of the Master; not as the chosen three, yet one as is given often the greater physical conditions to do and to carry out. One often spoken to for the reference to others, and this is particularly seen, especially, upon two occasions: In the feeding of the multitudes in the entrance to the city for the evening lodgement to keep the Passover. In the entering into the Garden on the last evening . . .

After the dispersing of the followers when persecutions came, the entity, Andrew, then went into Mesopotamia, and those countries where the entity felt that the learning of the Master was obtained, during the early education of the Master, and the travels of the Master, see?

Then, the entity remained true to that teaching, and brought *many* to the knowledge of God that *is* within every human physical being that seeks to

know how same manifests through the individual.
341-19

Literally hundreds of pages of follow-up reports and file notations make this one of the most extensive cases documented in the Cayce files. After attending Washington and Lee University and working as a librarian, [341] became manager of a psychical and spiritual research organization. Married in his thirties, he and his wife had a small son before he was called to serve in the military during World War II. After the war, he resumed his duties as manager of a research organization. Eventually, he and his wife had another son.

Because of his speaking abilities and his love for church work, he was made a church deacon in 1947 and would serve as a guest speaker in many churches throughout the rest of his life. In addition to his work as manager of the research organization, he did extensive lecture work throughout the country during the 1950s through the 1970s. At the same time, he was very active in his community, in his church, and as a leader in the Boy Scouts.

Because of his involvement with psychic ability, by the 1960s he had become a leading figure in the field of parapsychology. His lecture engagements expanded to become international in scope, and in 1964 his first book regarding parapsychology and the unconscious was published. That same year he was chosen as the leading citizen in his city. His work in lecturing, writing, speaking, and managing the research association continued until his death in 1982.

Anna
Luke 2:36-38
Case 1521[1]

Mentioned in the New Testament, Anna is regarded as a saintly woman who was married for only seven years before becoming a widow for the next seventy-seven years. Though elderly, she spent her time in the temple, praying and fasting and waiting for the coming of the Messiah. Known as a prophetess, when Mary and Joseph presented the baby Jesus at the temple, Anna announced publicly that Jesus was the Messiah and the fulfillment of all God's promises. She thanked God that she had lived long enough to see that prophecy fulfilled.

In 1938, parents of a one-week-old baby girl were told that their daughter had been Anna. The reading stated that their child was extremely determined and would always have its own way. To their amazement, the parents were also told that in addition to Anna, their baby had lived two additional lives of notoriety: one as Anne Boleyn, second wife of Henry VIII after he divorced Catherine of Aragon and broke with the Roman Catholic Church, and the other as Hannah, mother of the prophet Samuel. (See also "Hannah.")

> Before that we find the entity was in the land and period when there were those expectancies for the coming of the Lord, the Master, the promise of those influences in the experience of men!

---

[1]Edgar Cayce also told two other individuals that they had been "Anna" in the temple at the time of Jesus: a thirty-four-year-old woman in 1936, case [1222], and a fifty-five-year-old woman in 1941, case [2629]. Since three individuals were given the same incarnation, we have to assume one of several possibilities: (1) There was more than one Anna in the Temple who had an experience with Jesus when He was a child; (2) Edgar Cayce made a mistake; or (3) Gladys Davis, Cayce's secretary, made a mistake when taking down the past-life identity.

> The entity then was the prophetess Anna, that waited in the temple and held and blessed Him in the days when there was according to the law the presenting of, the purifying of the Mother by the material and the spiritual law of the people in that experience.
>
> The entity gained throughout that experience, though suffering in body, suffering in many of those things that arise from those activities in a materialistic world of a spiritual-*minded* individual given to a purpose and a cause that is in the spiritual and mental sense to be the source of redemption for the great numbers rather than the few. 1521-1

In addition to her intuition, in her incarnation in Palestine she had acquired a personal awareness of the presence of God. In ancient Egypt she had been with her present father and had assisted him in a rebellion against those in power. The parents were encouraged to develop their daughter's spiritual interests and were told that the child's present direction would be entirely dependent upon the guidance and upbringing she received.

Although raised in a Catholic home, her father, a writer of some reputation, had a great deal of frustration with many aspects of his religion. [1521]'s parents later obtained physical readings for their daughter on a variety of childhood ailments, including an unusual amount of hair that grew across the back of the child's neck and shoulders. As she grew to adulthood, [1521] maintained an interest in spirituality and would study both Catholicism and Judaism (her husband's religion).

At one point, [1521] became a very successful newspaper reporter. One of the last reports on file states that she and her husband had two sons and that she had just been accepted to law school.

Apsafar
Luke 2:7
Case 1196

Although not named in the Bible, Edgar Cayce stated that the owner of the inn to whom Joseph and the expectant mother had come for shelter was named Apsafar. (He was also given the name Abel-Tean, which may be accounted for by the fact that during this time rich with Roman, Hebrew, and Arabic customs many individuals possessed more than one name.) Rather than being cruel and turning the couple aside because there were no more rooms, as is related in the Bible, Cayce stated that Apsafar was actually an Essene who had been advised by the Essene leaders that Joseph and Mary would arrive. In order to protect the couple (and keep them from "the rabble" who had already taken up residence in the inn), Apsafar directed them to the very place of safety that had already been prepared for them.

In 1936, a fifty-eight-year-old railway commercial agent contacted Edgar Cayce about a health condition. In all, he would receive more than a dozen physical readings about his stiff joints, his problems with eliminations, and the pains in his abdomen. The condition would later be diagnosed as cholecystitis. When he obtained a life reading, he was told that he possessed high mental abilities and was swayed by both duty and sentiment. An emotionally passionate individual, he could be quick to anger but was just as quick to forgive. His life reading provided a number of past-life experiences.

During the time of the American Revolution, [1196] had served as a quartermaster for stores and supplies. Extremely helpful to his fellow soldiers, at the time he had also shown kindness and fellowship to any enemy that had been captured and held. He was encouraged to continue this manner of dealing with people which was best phrased as, "As ye do it unto these, the least of thy brethren, ye do it unto me." Previously, in France, he had assisted individuals in his capacity as one who planned routes, roads, and excursions into surrounding territories, often bringing "greater convenience" to isolated places. In an earlier life, he had been a leader of caravans involved with exchanging goods between Egyptian and Persian lands. In another incarnation in Egypt, he had also served in the capacity of counselor.

His previous lives had caused him to love travel, to desire to open up lines of communications among peoples, and to provide individuals with greater conveniences and material things in their home. He was told that he had been the innkeeper to whom Joseph and Mary had come when she was about to give birth:

> Much of that as has been recorded as we find is not so well, nor in keeping with that the entity did then—as Apsafar; who was of the Essenes, though of a Jewish descent, though a combination of the Jewish and the Grecian.
>
> For the entity then made a study of those peoples, knew of those things that had been foretold by the teachers of the Essenes, and made all preparations as near in keeping with what had been foretold as possible. 1196-2

During that same incarnation, Apsafar had often served as a counselor to those who sought advice regarding how to best deal with the various groups and political influences of the time. In that experience, his present wife had also been his daughter and she had been among the first to see the baby Jesus. Finally, [1196] was told that his talents in the present lay in communications or commerce and trade. He could excel in the line of imports and have a tremendous influence in the lives of many people.

After the reading, Mr. [1196] reported, "It is very, very interesting. Strange to say, often I have thought that I had at some time, at some place, known my present wife." Both he and his wife were thrilled with the information.

Follow-up reports indicate that in 1948 he visited A.R.E. and in 1952 wrote to inquire about information in the readings for a sinus problem he was experiencing. The last file notation is from 1959 when he submitted a change of address. No additional information is on file.

Ashtueil
Matthew 2
Case 256

According to the New Testament, Wise Men journeyed from the East following a star which they believed heralded the birth of the Christ child. King Herod had heard of them and summoned them to his court, requesting that once the child was discovered they tell him where the infant might be found. The Wise Men continued their journey to Bethlehem, found the babe, and offered gifts of gold, frankincense, and myrrh. Afterward, they were warned in a dream not to return to Herod; therefore, they traveled back to their country by another route. Although they were not specifically named in the Bible, Edgar Cayce gave two individuals life readings and stated that each had been one of the Wise Men: Ashtueil and Achlar. (See also "Achlar.")

An accounting teacher was told that he had exceptional abilities that could be applied in the present. He could use his talent with mathematics to excel in boat building, architecture, or aeronautics. Innately, he also possessed an aptitude for numerology, astrology, and astronomy that could be used to assist others. His past incarnations included an English monk during the Crusades. From that lifetime he had also possessed a talent with numbers and stars. In ancient Egypt he had been a mathematical genius who had studied the skies and was told, because of that incarnation, he was one of the few individuals alive who could understand Einstein's theory of relativity. He was also informed that he had been the Wise Man who had offered the gift of frankincense to the baby Jesus:

> In the one before this we find the entity was among those who were of the Wise Men coming into Jerusalem and to Bethlehem when the Master came into the earth. The entity then in the name Ashtueil, coming in from the mountains of what is now known as Arabia and India. The entity gained through this period in pointing out that through the various forces as were added in the experiences of man with that creation of forces necessary to keep the balance in the universal forces, the earth must bring forth that that would make man's balance of force with the Creative Energy as one, and the Son of Man appeared. The entity brought the frankincense and gave same to the Master at that period.
>
> 256-1

His talents lay in numbers, astrology, and in facilitating the mental abilities of others. Mr. [256] was encouraged to become the astrologer for Cayce's Association, providing progressive charts for the Association's membership. Over the years, he obtained a number of readings and became active in the Search for God® study group program. He requested readings for members of his family and married in 1937 at the age of thirty-nine. Unfortunately, three years later, Mr. [256], who had apparently been working on his car, died of carbon monoxide poisoning. His sister remained convinced that the death was not completely accidental and that someone had killed him. She wrote Mr. Cayce in 1941 to tell him that her dead brother had communicated with her, stating that he was doing fine and wished her to express his love and blessings to those he had known in life.

Barak
Judges 4, 5; Hebrews 11:32-34
Case 1710

Barak was a warrior who became the most important ally to Deborah, a prophetess and judge for Israel, in the struggle against the Canaanites. Barak was summoned by Deborah to bring ten thousand men to Mount Tabor in order to fight against the Canaanites. He agreed under the condition that she come with him. Deborah accompanied him and Barak's forces proved superior.

A twenty-four-year-old man, whose family had received a number of readings, was told that he had been Barak, an incarnation in which he had excelled at being able to place his faith in God. In a lifetime just previous to the present, he had served at Fort Dearborn, Chicago, as a teacher to youth as well as a customs director. In Rome, he had served as a centurion and a director of those who collected customs. Finally, in Atlantis, he had served as an emissary to other lands.

In the present, [1710] was informed that the career best suited for his abilities lay in the fields of machinery, electronics, mechanics, and especially aeronautics as long as he remained on the ground. When the young man asked about marriage, he was told that the greatest influence would come from his incarnation in the Holy Land and that he shouldn't contemplate marriage until he was twenty-eight or twenty-nine.

When [1710] was twenty-eight, he met and married a young woman who was told that she had been Deborah. (See also "Deborah.") A few months after their marriage, they obtained a joint reading on their lifetime as Barak and Deborah, which stated:

> As indicated there, they each had their definite activities; Deborah as the elder in the experience, and the prophetess—thus raised to a power or authority as a judge in Israel; to whom the people of the various groups, of that particular portion of Israel, went for the settling of their problems pertaining to their relationships one to another . . .
>
> Then did the entity Deborah appoint or call Barak to become the leader in the armed forces against the powers of Sisera [captain of the Canaanites] . . .
>
> As to the activities of Barak in those periods—there was something like some twelve years variation in the ages. Barak was also a family man, of the same tribe—though not of the same household as Deborah. Their activities, then, brought only the respect one for the other in their associations, their dealings and relationships with others. 1710-11

By working together, the reading assured the couple that they could again be helpful to others. In time, the couple would have four children.

Reports on file indicate that [1710] worked for the Martin Company and became trained on a variety of instruments involving aeronautics that were manufactured by Sperry. By 1957, he had started a successful contracting company, building roads, digging for underground utilities, and landscaping.

In 1967, [1710] died unexpectedly from a cerebral hemorrhage.

Bartimaeus
Mark 10:46-52; Luke 18:35-43
Case 2124

Bartimaeus was a well-known blind man who spent his time begging along the highway at the entrance to Jericho. In spite of the crowd's insistence that he remain silent when Jesus passed by, Bartimaeus repeatedly called out to be healed. It was because of his faith that he gained back his sight.

A fifty-four-year-old night watchman, who had previously obtained physical readings for himself and a life reading for his granddaughter, secured his own life reading in 1931. Not easily swayed by others, he was told that he had a mind of his own but managed to think first before speaking. He also had talent as a politician. His reading stated that just previous to the present lifetime, he had been an explorer and navigator from the Norse land. In ancient Egypt, he had been a builder and a politician. In Atlantis, he had also been a navigator. However, his most influential incarnation had been at the time of Jesus: "being in the name then of Bartimaeus, as walked by the way; being strong in body, yet lacking—through the activities of those with whom the body-entity then associated—in sight . . . " (2124-3)

Because of that lifetime, Cayce told [2124] that he maintained a deep interest in helping others with their own healing. That same year, he and his wife became a part of the first Search for God study group and the first prayer group. A year later, the couple withdrew from the Cayce work, deciding that they did not believe in reincarnation.

A file notation from 1940 states that the couple continued to speak very highly of Mr. Cayce, but still did not accept reincarnation. Mr. [2124] died in 1960 at the age of eighty-three.

Belshazzar
Daniel 5, 7:1, 8:1
Case 4609

Belshazzar was the son of the mighty king, Nebuchadnezzar, and the last king of Babylon before it was overtaken by the Persians. During a banquet he was giving to a thousand members of his royal court, a mysterious hand appeared and began writing a message upon the wall. No one at the banquet could decipher the message. The prophet Daniel was summoned, who explained that because of the king's misdeeds his reign was coming to an end and his kingdom would be divided. Belshazzar was slain by his enemies that very night.

In 1928, a thirty-nine-year-old crippled musician was told that his physical handicap was in response to his soul deciding to meet the misdeeds he had committed in his experience as Belshazzar.

> In the one before this we find the entity that ruler, that king in power, when the handwriting was given that those would be measured in the balance and those found wanting would be called to reckoning. The entity then lost through that experience, and in those forces that deal with the physical application or physical *result* of application of abilities we find the entity meriting many of those hardships through which the present experience brings to the entity; yet with all that, the love of harmony, that of the ability to listen ever for that warning, brings much to the entity, and—applied in the present sphere—may bring the development of the entity far along the way of gaining the more perfect understanding of the unison of forces as applied in the spiritual and mental realm, and of its application to physical forces in a material plane. 4609-1

Cayce told [4609] that in spite of his handicap, he was still held in awe both physically and mentally by many others. He had much to offer. However, too often [4609] judged others and found them lacking in some degree. Rather than keeping himself aloof, he was encouraged to make many lasting friendships, one of his talents. He was also encouraged to use his creative abilities to be of service to others. In addition to his lifetime as Belshazzar, in ancient Egypt he had been the chief musician responsible for working with the vibratory forces of healing. He had also been incarnate during the earliest periods of Atlantis.

With the exception of some correspondence between [4609] and Edgar Cayce the year of his reading, no additional follow-up reports are on file.

Benaiah

II Samuel 8:18, 20:23, 23:20, 22; I Kings 1-2, 4:4; I Chronicles 11:22-24, 18:17, 27:5-6
Case 2316

Benaiah was a loyal follower of David who proved himself extremely capable in military affairs, eventually becoming supreme commander of the army. His bravery was legendary. Once he even descended into a pit to do battle with a lion. He served as David's chief bodyguard and later assumed the same responsibilities under Solomon, never hesitating to put men of questionable loyalty to death.

In 1940, the parents of a sixteen-year-old boy requested a life reading for their son. Cayce told them that their child was an "unusual personality" and had various innate urges that would influence his life's direction. In addition to being deeply interested in mystical or psychical information, the boy had a well-developed imagination and was a gifted storyteller and writer. On the negative side, the boy was convinced that his judgment was superior to others and he also had the tendency to want to spend more money than he possessed.

Inclined to be moody and cynical, he discovered through his reading that his past lives had been quite varied. During the colonial period, [2316] had been a record keeper and an administrator of the law in Williamsburg, Virginia. During a lifetime with the Crusades in France, he had argued against attempting to impose French beliefs onto people from other lands. In ancient Egypt, he had assisted individuals with vocational guidance. He was told that one of the greatest mental influences in his present experience came from his military career in the Holy Land:

> The entity then was Benoni [Gladys Davis later noted that she believed she had erroneously written down the name and that because of the reference she felt the reading was actually referring to Benaiah], the leader or director of the army or the military forces of that great king; thus one whose judgments and activities were looked upon as being close to the king himself.
>
> The entity gained, the entity lost; yet we may see much in the characteristics and personality of the present entity from the activities of the entity *as* Benoni, the keeper of the military forces of Solomon, the king—if there will be made a close study of those activities. 2316-1

Cayce encouraged the boy's parents to give their son an education in the law and prepare him for a career in writing or in law and order. When they asked about their son's future, Cayce stated, "Depends upon the use to which he puts his abilities."

In 1943, according to the last notation on file, the boy's

father stated that [2316] had foregone his studies at Princeton University for a time because he was extremely interested in becoming a part of active service in the navy.

Benaiah, the Levite
II Chronicles 31:13
Case 3528

This Benaiah lived during the time of King Hezekiah (known for his many reforms) and for a time was given the position of overseeing the offerings presented in the temple.

A thirty-six-year-old bakery salesman, who read about Edgar Cayce in *There Is a River,* in 1943 obtained a life reading and was told that his tendency to become headstrong was due to his lifetime as Benaiah. At that time, he had apparently been taken into captivity by order of the king for gratifying his own selfish interests and forgetting the ways of the Lord. Although Benaiah later regretted his misdeeds, his banishment enabled him to become educated. His reading stated, "From that experience the entity learned to write. For as Benaiah, the entity was educated in the schools of those lands where the entity was taken as hostage." (3528-1) That ability to write remained with him in the present, and he was told that he could become "a writer of note" provided he overcome his propensity for sarcasm.

Additional past lives had occurred in colonial times when he had worked with the Native Americans to learn their customs as well as a lifetime during the time of the Mound Builders, when [3528] had acquired a respect for the soil and the preparation of foods. He was encouraged to focus his talents into composition and writing, even writing articles about food if he so desired.

His reading stated that it was due to his own sensitivity that he often appeared sarcastic and pessimistic. He was encouraged to be sincere, learning to control his temper and not say things that he really didn't mean. He was also told to focus his energies into learning how to apply spiritual principles in everyday life, learning his true relationship to the Creative Forces. By so doing, he would have the opportunity to work with writing.

Later reports suggest that [3528] found the information on spirituality in the Cayce information very helpful to him. In 1952, he filled out a follow-up questionnaire and stated that the reading's analysis of his abilities and tendencies had been "absolutely correct" and that he was "fundamentally in agreement with the reading—especially as to basic character traits." At the same time, he admitted that his own "laziness" and "lack of will" had caused him to do nothing about pursuing writing. He still confessed to being sarcastic, hardheaded, and capable of "flying off the handle" easily.

No additional follow-up reports are on file.

Benaiah, the Pirathonite

II Samuel 23:30; I Chronicles 11:31, 27:14

Case 3001

This Benaiah was considered one of the thirty valiant men of David. He served as a division commander for the army, going on active duty during the eleventh month of each year.

A fifty-two-year-old business owner, involved in the textile industry, was told that his love of "clothing, woolens, textiles of all natures, especially skins [and] furs" had originated in his most recent life as a British citizen who had settled in New York during the American Revolution. He had also been among the tribe of Levi in a lifetime in the Holy Land, where he had gained spiritually because of his attempt to apply spiritual principles in the face of external obstacles. His abilities as a leader and the lifetime of greatest influence, however, were due to his incarnation as Benaiah:

> For, the entity then was Benaiah. Hence those inclinations or tendencies; for the individual entity would not be called a religious man, and yet there is the adherence to—or the desire of information, knowledge, or that in which the entity interests self—in comparative religions, comparative philosophy, comparative things having to do with the mental and spiritual influences in the lives of men. Yet it also makes the entity a hard taskmaster.
>
> 3001-1

Mr. [3001] was told that he also possessed abilities with "mechanical things, or those things prepared by mechanical things" and could write, if he chose to do so. As long as he overcame his own hardheadedness and treated others as he would choose to act toward his Creator, he would find joy in life and understand the purpose for which he had come into the earth. He was encouraged to begin learning how he could serve those around him.

The only report on file states that Mr. [3001] and his wife were planning to attend the A.R.E. membership Congress in 1943.

Benjamin

Genesis 35:15-29, 42-43, 45-46, 49; Exodus 1:1-7; Deuteronomy 33; I Chronicles 2:1-2, 7:1-7
Case 221

Benjamin was the second son born to Jacob and Rachel, his father's favorite wife who died shortly after Benjamin was born. After Joseph was sold into slavery,

Benjamin became his father's favorite. When there was famine in Canaan, Jacob reluctantly sent Benjamin and his brothers into Egypt to buy grain. When it was finally revealed that Joseph was not dead but had become prime minister of Egypt, Jacob and his sons all moved to Egypt. (See also "Reuben.")

In 1940, in a reading given to the Glad Helpers Prayer Group, Cayce discussed the activity of the body's endocrine system and the important influence parents played during conception in attracting a soul into the earth. In a brief side comment in this regard, Cayce stated that the soul that had been Saul had also incarnated as Benjamin, the second son of Jacob and Rachel. (See also "Saul" and "Seth.")

Boaz

(also known as Booz)
Ruth 2-4; I Kings 7:21; I Chronicles 2:11-12; Matthew 1:5; Luke 3:32
Case 2694

Boaz was a wealthy landowner who lived near Bethlehem. He took pity on a young woman named Ruth, who scoured fields that had already been picked looking for something to eat. His kindness eventually led to their marriage. (See also "Ruth" and "Naomi.") Their son became King David's grandfather.

In 1927, a thirty-one-year-old Realtor and businessman obtained a life reading. He was told that in addition to a developed intellect he also allowed himself to be governed by love and sentiment—even to his own undoing. A true diplomat in the handling of delicate situations, he often placed others' needs before his own. Cayce told him that throughout his life he would have influence over the lives of many and be in control of substantial amounts of money. Since he honored truth above all things, his reading stated that he could have excelled as a lawyer.

In past lives, he had lived in France during the time of Richelieu, where he had been a member of the church aristocracy and was very disappointed by Richelieu's activities. During the time of Nero, he had been a soldier in the court, yet managed to act and live for the good of others. In ancient Greece, he had worked on sailing ships. In ancient Egypt, he had been among those who had attempted to bring together a divided people. His lifetime as Boaz could be of the greatest help to him in the present:

> In the one before this we find in one that was made known in the lands of the day when the entity rose to position, power, wealth, in the name Boaz, and the entity then brought much good to the peoples of that day, especially in the reclaiming of lands for those oppressed, or for those who had lost same, through the laws of redemption of lands that were taken for debt or for the reason of exile, giving especially to the peoples through that offspring that brought David in the land—and the entity gained through this experience, as there was much to the tenets followed, and the expressions of action by the entity through the experience. In the urge as is seen, is that especially toward real estate—for the entity wrote the first advertisement for sale of lands in this age. 2694-1

His talent with real estate and assisting many others came to fruition in subsequent years when he served in various executive posts for the FHA and, as his life reading had predicted, [2694] had control over vast sums of money. No additional reports are on file.

Caleb

Numbers 13:1-33; 14; 26:65; 32:10-13; 34:16-29; Deuteronomy 1:34-36; Joshua 14, 15, 21:12; Judges 1, 3:9; I Samuel 25:3, 30:14; I Chronicles 2, 4:15, 6:56
Case 1292

Representing the tribe of Judah, Caleb was one of the twelve spies that Moses sent to scout the Promised Land of Canaan. Only Caleb and Joshua brought back a report encouraging the conquest of Canaan as had been decreed by God, while the rest of the Israelites were afraid to follow God's command. Because only Joshua and Caleb had remained faithful, they were the only two among the original members of the twelve tribes sent into the wilderness who were allowed to enter the Promised Land. After the conquest of Canaan, Caleb was given Hebron and the area surrounding it. Later, he promised his daughter Achsah's hand in marriage to whomever would assist him in conquering his lands.

Parents of a three-year-old boy obtained a life reading for their son on the same day that the boy's father received a physical reading. Told that their boy was sensitive, stubborn, idealistic, expressive, and high-strung, they were encouraged to always reason with their child, frequently explaining to him the rationale behind things. Because he would be inclined to act and think quickly, the parents were encouraged to provide [1292] with basic spiritual principles in his upbringing.

In his most recent past life, the boy had been involved with law and order during the early settlement of California. From that same experience, he had also developed an interest in new fields of activity or study, such as science, innovations, and music. At the same time, however, the California experience had given him an innate fear of firearms and explosions. During a lifetime at the height of the Roman Empire, [1292] oversaw tax collections for portions of the empire in Greece, Turkey, and Palestine. Cayce said that the boy possessed abilities as an orator as well as in law and order, and would be given some measure of authority by the latter portion of his present life. In fact, the reading stated that it would even be possible for their son to be a United States Supreme Court judge.

The parents were told that their son had also served as a diplomat in ancient Egypt, whereas in Atlantis he had misused spiritual principles for material gain. The boy's most influential life, however, had been as an Israelite who had left the bondage of Egypt to find the Promised Land:

> Hence the entity was ever looked to as one to be counseled with, as one to be looked upon as a leader, as a sage in Israel; Caleb, then as the companion of Joshua, with the children of Judah that made for the cleansing of the land for that which became the Holy City; that has meant, did mean so much in the experience of the people as a people and of the world; that has had, does have so great a mental influence upon the world today, as it ever will.
>
> For as then the entity founded same, its purposes, its desires, its activities were in the law of the *living* God, that enjoined all those who would to draw nigh unto Him . . .
>
> For those laws are ever those things that in the experience of individuals in the material world make for a fortress of *strength,* as they did for the entity in that sojourn. 1292-1

Cayce also stated that the boy's mother had been his daughter during his experience as Caleb. (See also "Achsah.")

As to the boy's future, it was dependent upon his training during the "formative years." He was encouraged to be trained in the laws of God as well as law "in relation to other lands—or *international* law." In addition to reason, they were to guide [1292] by precept and example. By their doing so, their son would have the opportunity to offer much to many people.

Within eight months of the boy's reading, his father died. The last notation on file is from 1952. At the time, [1292] was eighteen years old, and his mother requested a copy of his life reading. In appreciation she wrote, "Thank you so much for the copy . . . It is most interesting to me since he is now a young man and he also will enjoy following his life's reading as the years go by."

No additional reports are on file.

Cleopas
Luke 24:13-35
Case 870

Cleopas was one of two disciples who walked along the road to Emmaus, discussing the fact that their master, Jesus, had been crucified. Suddenly, Jesus appeared to them, but neither recognized Him until after they had eaten a meal together. Immediately afterward, Jesus disappeared and the two ran back to Jerusalem to tell the apostles about the Resurrection. It was while the two related their tale that Jesus appeared to the entire group and tried to put His followers at ease by saying: "Peace be unto you."

In 1935, the mother of a fifteen-year-old boy obtained a life reading for her son, requesting information about their past-life connections as well as the name of the college he should attend. The college the reading suggested was Yale, and the past-life connections included Egypt and Palestine. The lifetime in Palestine continued to be an important influence in the boy's present life:

> The entity was among those that gathered with those of His followers, and was among those that became the closer disciples of the Master; remaining with those throughout the greater portion of the teachings of same, and was the brother-in-law of Peter, that one that became as the spokesman for those of the twelve that gathered as His material representatives in the earth.
>
> Then the entity was in the name Cleopas, and the husband of Cleo—or the father of Mark. In the experience the entity gained throughout . . . 870-1

During the early settling of Pennsylvania, [870] had been one of the first individuals born in the new land. In that incarnation he had become a teacher and now possessed the ability to lead groups of people, especially as a mediator or a counselor. In Persia, he had been one of the sons of King Croesus, although not the heir, and was responsible for keeping his father's records regarding trade and commerce. From that experience came a desire to preserve a record of the activities of both groups and individuals. A lifetime in ancient Egypt had seen him as one of those involved in the establishment of various settlements throughout different portions of the known world.

Cayce stated that although [870]'s astrological influences might appear "adverse," from a soul perspective they entailed a great deal of development. He was told that "the next three and a half to five years" would provide for the most interesting experiences in his current lifetime. Told that he possessed a great deal of vision, as well as mental and emotional abilities, he was encouraged to pursue the arts, physical fitness, or diplomacy.

According to the reports on file, [870] was killed in a

tragic automobile accident in September 1940.

Cornelius
Acts 10
Case 1848

The story of the conversion to Christianity of Cornelius, the Roman centurion, had enormous implications for the early Church. Previously, only Jews who followed the rites of diet and circumcision could be considered for admission into the faith. While praying, Cornelius had a vision in which an angel told him to send for Peter. At the same time, Peter had a vision in which he was told to consider no one as impure. While Peter was visiting Cornelius's house, the Holy Spirit descended upon the gathering, causing Peter to realize that God was not limiting Christianity to the Jews but enabling the Gentiles to be converted as well. That same day, Cornelius and his household were baptized.

In 1939, a fifty-seven-year-old United States senator requested a life reading in order to assist him in making certain choices. Cayce began the reading by stating that many of [1848]'s incarnations had influenced "man's experience in dealing with his fellow man." The outstanding lifetime, however, had been as Cornelius, the first Roman official to openly embrace the tenets of Jesus.

> Before that we find the experience which is indicated as the outstanding activity of the entity—when the entity was the centurion, the keeper or the officer of the Roman forces stationed in Caesarea.
>
> There the entity, through the associations with those who had come in personal contact with the man of Galilee, began his seeking—through prayer—to know what was man's relationship to his Maker.
>
> Then there was the receiving of the vision as the

> warning that he, Cornelius, was to send for one [Peter] that would acquaint him with those truths which had been proclaimed by that representative of the heavenly kingdom.
>
> And those activities of the entity in accepting, in experiencing the outpouring and the call through the activity of the spirit of truth, made for that *great* change which came in the governing of that land; and the modifying of the authority of those who were put in power through the activities of the authorities in Rome; making it possible, with those of its fellows, that there would come the great opportunities for man in every walk of life to become acquainted with those truths that are a part of man's heritage through the promises of the Creative Forces in man's experience. 1848-1

In the present, Senator [1848] was told that he possessed the ability to remind individuals everywhere of their connection to the Creative Forces. His past lives included that of a Norse explorer who had championed freedom for all peoples. Previously, he had been a Greek who had journeyed into Persia in order to learn spiritual truths. As an Atlantean, he had served as a diplomat and a *"messenger of peace"* between Egypt and Atlantis.

His reading stated that he found himself in his present position in order to serve as a peacekeeper, proclaiming peace "through brotherly love and kindness and gentleness, and patience." He could be helpful in this regard to those in the highest authority. He was told that his strengths included honesty, integrity, justice, mercy, and truth. He was encouraged to remain in his present occupation as a representative of his fellow humans.

When he asked about the possibility of being elected the next president of the United States, Cayce stated that it could happen provided he maintained his own principles and not subvert them to the ideas of others. When [1848] asked about the destiny of the United States in regard to the European conflict, he was informed that unless Senator [1848] or someone like him became the next president, "*turmoils* and strifes must increase."

One of the only direct reports on file is from 1975, an obituary noting the death of [1848] at the age of ninety-two. The report states that he was "one of the most powerful isolationists in the U.S. Senate before World War II . . . served four terms beginning in 1922 and lost a bid for re-election in 1946 largely on his opposition to U.S. intervention in World War II."

Cyrus

II Chronicles 36:22-23; Ezra 1, 3:7, 4:3-5, 5, 6:3, 14; Isaiah 44:28, 45:1; Daniel 1:21, 6:28, 10:1

Case 2795

Cyrus the Great (ca. 553-529 B.C.) was king of Persia who founded the Persian Empire by overthrowing the Median Empire and conquering the kingdom of Babylon. He became a hero to the Jews by allowing them to return from their exile in Babylon to their native Israel in order to rebuild the temple. At its height, his empire stretched from Afghanistan to the Mediterranean.

In 1942, a twenty-eight-year-old man received a life reading in order to discern the purpose for his present incarnation. The reading told him that because of his various past-life influences, the outcome of his life could follow one of three difference courses: "a complete failure, a mediocre career, or that which will outshine most of its fellows." He was advised to become a messenger for spiritual principles and in the process, "*unifying* man to his oneness with that Creative Force we call God." Cayce stated that he would have just such an opportunity to become a messenger of brotherly love in his thirty-fourth or thirty-fifth year.

Mr. [2795]'s past incarnations included an experience in France in which he had often been confused about whether he was best suited for taking the spiritual, the mental, or the material approach to life. In the Holy Land, he had been the son of an Essene leader and was often afraid of being persecuted for his associations. His lifetime of greatest growth had been as Cyrus the Great:

> The entity was the Persian and Chaldean king [Cyrus the Great] who moved first to declare the rights of each group and of each nation to worship according to the dictates of their own conscience; and issued those first decrees for the return of those of Judah to the rebuilding of the temple . . . 2795-1

From that same experience, [2795] maintained an interest in those things which enabled individuals to find spiritual, economic, and political freedom.

Earlier lives had included that of a spiritual and economic leader in Egypt, in which he had lost hold of his spiritual beliefs; and in Atlantis, when his work with energy waves had inadvertently led to one of the destructions of the continent. In another Atlantean incarnation, he had helped to unify spiritual principles for their practical use.

Cayce stated that [2795]'s talents could be guided into positive or negative channels. He was encouraged to get an understanding of his true relationship to the Creative Forces and to direct his energies into those fields that could unify and benefit humankind.

Follow-up reports indicate that [2795] was extremely interested in ancient civilizations, especially Lemuria and Atlantis. He studied the readings on these subjects and hoped to discover how to harness the ever-present energy of the universe. According to a file notation from

Gladys Davis, he continued to correspond periodically with Hugh Lynn Cayce into the 1950s.

No additional reports are on file.

Deborah
Judges 4-5
Case 2803

Deborah was a prophetess and judge of Israel who was looked up to as one who unified the tribes before there was one kingdom. She summoned the warrior Barak to bring ten thousand men to Mount Tabor in order to fight against the Canaanites. Together they defeated the army and its leader, and their victory was immortalized in song.

A twenty-three-year-old restaurant hostess was told that her present boyfriend had been her protector during a lifetime in the Holy Land. They were advised to establish a home together in the present, for she had been Deborah and he had been Barak. (See also "Barak.")

> Before that the entity was in the Promised Land, during those eras of the Judges in the land.
>
> The entity then was that prophetess who enabled Barak to bring freedom to those peoples. While the associations and companion were of another group, the entity chose Barak as the leader of God's forces in the delivery of the peoples from Sisera [captain of the Canaanites] and those hordes that were making those people in that period as slaves.
>
> Read oft the song, then, of Deborah, as thine *own* composition, as thy tribute to man, to his efforts when guided by the divine as indicated there.
>
> 2803-2

Her most recent incarnation had been as the wife of Stonewall Jackson during the Civil War. From that period, she was inclined to have an attitude of self-belittlement. She had been an English woman during one of the wars between Spain and had lost her sons to the conflict. During another incarnation she had been a follower of Jesus in Palestine and had come to know both Peter and Paul. From that lifetime, she maintained an understanding of spiritual laws. In Egypt, she had been among those who had assisted in the establishment of family homes.

Cayce told her that because her experience with home life had not always been a positive one, she was encouraged to establish a home and to raise a family. Ms. [2803] and her boyfriend married within four months of her life reading. During the first year of their marriage she wrote, "We have had a great deal of happiness in being together. We are so glad and thankful we had our readings to guide us."

In time, the couple would have four children. Unfortunately her husband died from a cerebral hemorrhage in 1967. In 1970, she wrote that she was getting married again to a rear admiral. The last file notation is from April 1973 when it states that the rear admiral had died from a self-inflicted wound.

Dinah

Genesis 30:21; 34; 46:15

Case 951

Dinah was the daughter of Jacob and Leah. Because of her beauty, she was seduced by Shechem, the son of Hamor, one of the chiefs of the Canaanites. Although Shechem was anxious to marry Dinah and pay a dowry, his violation of her caused her brothers, Simeon and Levi, to plot revenge. They told Shechem and his people that they would consent to marriage provided all of Shechem's men underwent circumcision. The men consented and on the third day after the operation, while they were still recuperating, Simeon and Levi attacked the city and massacred its people, including Hamor and Shechem. Afterward, Dinah was taken back to her family.

In 1939, a twenty-four-year-old woman requested a life reading. In spite of her young age, she had already come to Mr. Cayce previously for help with arthritis. Feeling very much better, she obtained a life reading and asked, in part, about her marital prospects. Cayce assured her that a husband would present himself through the normal course of events. In the meantime, she was to continue to work on her physical, mental, and spiritual well-being.

Her past lives included a sojourn in colonial America, where she had assisted young people in preparing themselves for the mental and physical demands of pioneer life. In France, she had been incarnate as a man during the Crusades and had acquired a love of pomp, ceremony, and all kinds of food, which Cayce stated was the cause of some of her health problems in the present. During a lifetime in England and Scotland, [951] had been frequently courted (and fought over) by the various groups of those in power. In Egypt, she had been a soothsayer who could forecast by the stars and read the movements of the sand. She had also had an earlier life in ancient Egypt as one who had been raised to be pure in body and physically perfect. Her incarnation in the Promised Land had followed the lifetime in ancient Egypt:

> There we find the entity was among the children of Jacob, and the daughter in that experience—one among twelve sons; and she whom Shechem sought, and over which much turmoil to Levi and Simeon was brought, owing to the conditions which arose through those activities as they journeyed in that land from the Arabian . . .
>
> Then the name was Dinah. 951-4

The reading stated that [951] possessed a great many powers of attraction. She also appreciated everything associated with beauty, color, symmetry, nature, and creation. Her life was destined to include an interest in spirituality, intuition, and mysticism. Cayce advised her to wear a pearl upon her body because it would continue to assist her physically. She was encouraged to pursue an occupation that would enable her to help others with physical exercise, recreation, or dancing. In time, she could focus upon creating a home for herself and her family-to-be.

Immediately after receiving the reading, [951]'s mother wrote: "It is all very interesting and I hope very helpful to her as she travels along. Thank you so much." That same year, [951] wrote and thanked Edgar Cayce for all the help he had provided her, physically, mentally, and spiritually.

In 1940, she started studying astrology and numerology and attended the annual membership Congress at A.R.E. The following year, [951] received another physical reading and was encouraged to go to the California mountains for her health, advice which she followed. While in California, she met a young lieutenant and married him. They had a daughter in 1943 but divorced in 1956.

In 1955, her mother again wrote Cayce's Association and expressed her thanks for the readings: "I am ashamed of myself for not writing long ago, intended to many times; thought of you all often, for instance when [951] had her thirty-sixth birthday (she is forty-one now), which doubled her life from her first Cayce reading at age eighteen when she was so sick and we were so worried."

In response to a query about whether she had ever worn the pearl recommended in her reading, [951] stated that although she had only worn it for a couple of years she attributed its use to the reason that "I have had fair health all these years." The final report is from 1967 when she wrote to tell Gladys Davis that she was working as a bookkeeper and still living in California, where the climate was helpful to her asthma and emphysema.

Elam
Ezra 2:31; Nehemiah 7:34
Case 900

After the reign of King Nebuchadnezzar when the Jews were allowed to return from their exile in Babylon, Elam was among those who came into Jerusalem and assisted in the rebuilding of the city.

Among the individuals who would have the greatest impact upon the work of Edgar Cayce were two Jewish stockbrokers, brothers, who underwrote the construction of the Cayce Hospital and enabled the Cayce family to move to Virginia Beach. (See also "Jude.") The eldest was self-certain, intelligent, and wealthy, and would personally obtain more readings that any other individual in the six-and-a-half years he was involved with the Association—an astonishing 468!

His life reading told him that he would excel in mental and financial affairs. Although he was extremely intelligent and self-motivated, he was encouraged to strive to work with others cooperatively—an exercise that would provide him with the best "results" in his present incarnation. His past lives included an incarnation as Achilles in Greece—a true historical person, according to Cayce. In that incarnation he had been responsible for giving freedom to the common people. Prior to his lifetime as Achilles, he had been one of those who had assisted in the rebuilding of Jerusalem:

> In the one before this we find of short duration,

> and in that of Elam who builded on the wall in the rebuilding of the Holy City, when the entity then returned with the chosen people and builded on and over the South Gate, then a defender and builder at the same time. Again we find those about the entity who now are in the earth's plane, yet not associated with same at present, or as yet. Will be. In the personality as is shown in the present, the desire to build and to give account of the labors done in mind or body, and capable of showing the effects of those buildings. Though the entity may be adverse at times to the advice of others, yet ever capable of showing results from the endeavors of the body, or mind, yet not carrying that "I told you so" with such conditions. 900-38

Prior to his incarnation in the Holy Land, he had been a native scribe among the Egyptian people and eventually rose to a place of leadership. From that lifetime he had acquired a love for the human mind and an understanding of humanity's relationship to God. Later readings would tell him that at the time he had "occupied the position of a Jefferson to the Declaration of Independence to the peoples in the religion and in the civil sense . . . " (900-275) Because of that past-life influence, in the present he was told that he could excel in writing, especially as he attempted to explain spiritual truths to others.

The challenge for Mr. [900] in this life was to apply the achievements he had accomplished over the physical/ mental realms and bring a new understanding of *oneness* and spirituality to the world. For a time, he headed up the work of Cayce's Association, becoming its chief financial backer and the builder of the Cayce Hospital. Extremely interested in higher education, he also founded Atlantic University. Unfortunately, due to personality conflicts and jealousy, [900] would later withdraw from the Association. In time, he would also lose his fortune.

In 1954, Mr. [900] died of a heart attack.

Elisha
I Kings 19; II Kings 2-9, 13
Case 2547

Originally the son of a wealthy landowner, Elisha became the servant and adopted son to the great prophet Elijah, who had followed God's instructions to find the young man. Shortly after joining the group of Elijah's disciples, Elisha became recognized as the prophet's successor, succeeding him after Elijah's ascension into heaven. Not realizing the magnitude of his power, immediately after receiving a "double portion" of his master's abilities, Elisha cursed forty-two children for making fun of his baldness. The curse caused two bears to come out of the woods and kill all of the children.

Elisha is known for his work as an advisor to kings as well as for the fact that he performed more miracles than any other individual in the Old Testament. His miracles included feeding a multitude with just a few barley loaves and corn, healing a man of leprosy, raising a child from the dead, causing an iron ax to lift from a river bottom, and filling a poor widow's vessels with oil. After his death, the very touch of his bones revived a man who had accidentally been buried in his sepulcher.

In 1941, Edgar Cayce gave one of his most remarkable life readings, promising the parents of a four-year-old boy that—provided their child was guided aright—it would be possible for their son to manifest the Christ Consciousness in the earth. The reading stated that the boy had often been responsible for the manifestation of spiritual truths in the earth and could bring much help and assistance to humankind.

Told that the boy could be an "extremist" in his expressions, words, and activities, Cayce recommended spiritual training and guidance, acquainting the child especially with the stories in the Old and New Testaments. Through a number of his incarnations in the earth, [2547] had acquired a deep personal relationship with the Creator and had learned how to manifest those principles in the earth. His present spiritual potential was nearly limitless.

In his most recent life, the child had been the Protestant reformer, Thomas Campbell, who had desired to unify Protestant thought. As a young boy during that lifetime, Cayce claimed that [2547] had been able to see and communicate with elementals and fairies. Remarkably, the parents were also told that their child had been Noah, the patriarch of the Deluge. (See also "Noah.") A third notable life had been as Elisha, Elijah's successor:

> For, before that the entity was that one upon whom the mantle of Elijah fell—who in his material activity performed more unusual acts, or miracles, that are only comparable with the Master Himself.
>
> The entity then as Elisha brought into the experience much that was of the unusual in expression.
>
> 2547-1

The reading saw great promise for the child's future and emphasized the important responsibility held by the parents, especially during their son's formative years.

Unfortunately, only a few follow-up reports are on file. In 1957, friends of the family informed the Association that [2547] had married. Apparently, [2547] and his wife were very active in their Protestant faith (Baptist) and in religious education. By this time, [2547] had chosen the grocery business as his profession. According to the family friend, he was very orthodox and did not appear open to such topics as reincarnation.

In 1963, an uncle reported that [2547] had become manager of a large supermarket chain in the small Southern town where he lived.

Elizabeth
Luke 1
Case 2156

Elizabeth and her husband, Zacharias, were devout Jews who were childless. In their old age, the angel Gabriel appeared to Zacharias and told him that he and his wife were to have a son. Because Zacharias did not believe, he was struck dumb and was unable to speak until after the baby's birth. As prophesied by the angel, Elizabeth became pregnant. During her pregnancy, her cousin, the Virgin Mary, visited her. Upon Mary's arrival, Elizabeth somehow knew that her cousin was carrying the Messiah. Mary resided with the couple during the early portion of her pregnancy. In time, Elizabeth gave birth to a son, who would grow to become John the Baptist.

Parents of a four-and-a-half-year-old girl obtained a reading for their daughter seeking information on their child who displayed a remarkable psychic talent. According to family friends, as soon as the child had begun to speak, she had been able to utter "the most amazing prophecies" about the future. In one instance, [2156] and her mother were sitting at the rear of a bus. The woman had just removed her daughter's leggings and overshoes and had convinced the girl to take a nap. Suddenly, the child jumped to her feet and demanded to have her winter attire put back on. The mother obliged and had no sooner finished when the whole rear end of the bus burst into flames. The bus was stopped in the midst of a heavy snowstorm, and everyone got out to safety.

Confirming that the little girl was a very special soul, Cayce stated that the child was even sensitive to the thoughts of others. Her psychic ability was traced to a number of previous incarnations, including one as a prophetess. In ancient Egypt, [2156] had worked with music and dance in the Temple Beautiful, teaching individuals how to prepare their bodies to be channels for the manifestation of spiritual principles in the earth. During the period of the early Church, the child had lived as Cecilia, the patron saint of music and musicians, known for her virginity, her distribution of possessions to the poor, and her martyrdom. Most notably, the child's parents were told that their daughter had been the mother of John the Baptist:

> Then again, before that, we find the entity was in that period from which the greater hope may be expressed; as Elizabeth, the mother of him of whom the Master said, "Among them that are born of woman there hath not risen a greater than John the Baptist."
>
> So, as the entity was a chosen vessel, a chosen channel for that one who *proclaimed* the day of the Lord to be at hand, the entity now—manifested in that body known as or called [2156]—may indeed be kept as a channel, by those about the entity, that it, too, may arouse and bring the consciousness in the minds of many that the day of the Lord is indeed at hand.
>
> For, whosoever will may come and take of the cup, even as He. For as He hath promised to stand in the places of those who are discouraged, disconsolate, who have lost a vision, lost hope—so may this entity be that channel through which *many* may take hope, many may be aroused to the awareness that the Lord is nigh, that He standeth at the door of thy consciousness, that ye may be awakened! 2156-1

The child's parents were advised to raise their daughter in as stable an environment as possible. Her intuition could develop further where it would eventually provide much assistance to humankind. Because of her innate abilities, Cayce stated that [2156] could become a great healer, both as a counselor and with the use of laying on of hands. The child would also possess musical talents that could be of assistance to herself and others both mentally and spiritually.

According to the reports on file, the child's mother was very impressed with her daughter's psychic talent, sometimes bringing together groups of people to which her daughter could make her prognostications. The father was not supportive in this and—according to the mother—had done "everything under the sun to combat [it]." The parents later separated and the child went to live with her father, where she abandoned her psychic work.

By 1963, [2156] had married and was living in Pennsylvania with her husband. At the time, both were involved in a wholesale distributing business.

No additional reports are on file.

Esdrela
Mark 1:29-31; Luke 4:38-39
Case 1541

After Jesus had gathered together some of His apostles and had been teaching in the synagogue in Capernaum, He entered into the house of Simon Peter and Andrew. There, Simon Peter's mother-in-law was very sick with a terrible fever. Jesus took her by the hand and healed her instantly. Afterward, she arose from her sick bed and began preparing some food and drink for her house guests. According to Edgar Cayce, the woman's name was Esdrela.

A sixty-two-year-old housewife and former grade

school teacher obtained physical readings as well as a life reading because of her daughter who had become very much involved in the Cayce work. For a time, she had also managed a flower business. A devout Baptist, she was a beautiful woman in many respects. Her one shortcoming was that she professed an intense hatred of Catholics and the Catholic Church. The animosity was traced to a life she had lived during the time of the apostles Peter and Paul, when she had seen firsthand what the antagonism between these two men had done to the early Church. Mrs. [1541] was told that she had been Peter's mother-in-law:

> For, the entity was among those of the group called the holy women, or those that saw, that knew many of the associations with the disciples, the apostles, and the helpful, direct influence of the Master Himself.
>
> For, the entity then was the mother of Peter's wife, once healed by the Master Himself.
>
> Those periods brought to the entity the closer associations through the latter periods of the activity. For, being healed as it were, physically, by the Master Himself, the entity's sojourn in the earth was long and varied, and would make a book in itself.
>
> The entity's ability to write in the present should be manifested, especially in the stories as concerning the life of the Master as might be read by children. For, these the entity would be able to do; as it brought through those experiences the channel through which the early church attracted others; as many lived and drew upon those truths as illustrated by the entity.
>
> During that experience the entity had *two* activities; the growing of plants, especially adaptable for the healing of the body, and flowers; and also the

> ministering to the sick. Not as a nurse—rather as a comforter. For the entity at periods acted in the capacity as a hired mourner, as was the custom of that period.
>
> The name then was Esdrela. 1541-11

During the course of her reading, Mrs. [1541] learned that she had known many members of her present family in her life just previous when she had lived in Fort Dearborn (Chicago). There, she had worked in the same dance hall as one of her daughters. In ancient Egypt, she had been a teacher, preparing those who were being sent as emissaries to other lands. She was encouraged to become active in any field of service that enabled her to be about her "Father's business," most notably writing, teaching, or homemaking. She was also encouraged to forgive others—just as she would like to be forgiven—and to turn away any wrath that presented itself.

Because of her daughter's involvement in the Cayce work, Mrs. [1541] and various family members have literally hundreds of pages of follow-up reports on file. During the course of one report, her daughter [1523] states:

> Of all the problems my mother has struggled with in this incarnation, perhaps the one dealing with Catholicism has caused the most heartache. When one of my brothers married a Catholic girl, mother remarked that she could face death with less difficulty. Yet this sister-in-law is perhaps more loved [than] any of the others . . . Another point—most interesting—was the mention of mother as a hired mourner. Once we went to a funeral—rather out of respect for the family of a neighbor. I noticed mother's expression and was astounded, for she seemed to be suffering greatly in grief of a loss—as

may have been expected at the funeral of a family member. I spoke to her about it later and she laughed, saying that she wasn't in the least aware of feeling grieved.

I have also observed her minister to the sick, both neighbors and family. Her mere presence brings strength and help to all. You can sense the feeling of peace and well-being that comes with her, and know instantly when she leaves. As she has grown older, her beauty has increased. Naturally, you might say in my eyes, but always there is someone mentioning to me—"how beautiful your mother is." "I only hope that I can be as beautiful as she when I grow old."

Because Mrs. [1541]'s reading had recommended writing spiritual stories for children, she attempted it on a number of occasions because of her daughter's encouragement but never felt that she had a true talent. In 1950, she and her husband celebrated their fiftieth wedding anniversary with family and friends.

In 1957, Mrs. [1541] suffered from a stroke, making it difficult for her to think or make decisions. Although her hands became quite weak, she was able to continue feeding herself. Her husband died in 1962 after a short illness, and she lived until 1964, dying at the age of eighty-five. Her daughter would later note that had it not been for her mother's sense of humor, the older woman would have undoubtedly become very depressed.

Esther
Esther 2, 4-9
Case 1298

Raised by her cousin Mordecai, Esther was an orphaned Jewish girl who rose to prominence because of her beauty. During the reign of King Ahasuerus, the king's wife, Vashti, was deposed for refusing to follow her husband's commands. (See also "Vashti.") As a result, Esther was chosen to take the queen's place at state banquets, eventually becoming his wife. Meanwhile, because Mordecai had refused to bow down before Haman, the king's chief minister, at the gate to the palace, Haman convinced the king that all Jews were subversive and needed to be annihilated. (See also "Haman.") At great personal risk, Esther intervened and reminded the king how the Jews had served him. King Ahasuerus agreed, changed his mind, then commanded that Haman and his sons be executed instead. This occasion of Jewish deliverance is commemorated as the feast of Purim.

A forty-three-year-old businesswoman's life reading began with the statement, "What a record!" Interested in metaphysics and involved with imports, she was told that her greatest abilities lay in the fields of writing, teaching, and lecturing. In these areas she could awaken the consciousness of others to spiritual truths.

In her life just previous to the present, [1298] was told that she had been among the Mound Builders, settling in portions of Alabama and Florida. From that experience, she had gained an appreciation for the Divine that resided within every individual. Previous to her American incarnation, she had been wife to the king in Persia:

> Hence the entity's close associations with that which made for that plea to the King, "Let my people go!"
>
> The entity then was Esther to Ahasuerus, close with those activities that have made for that upon which a peoples have worshipped not the individual but the purposes as wrought in the heart and activities of an individual, as directed by a man of God—Mordecai!

> Those brought in the experience of the entity the closer concept of the ideals, and yet the very act and fact that the entity itself enjoyed not those privileges of seeing the re-establishing of the temple, nor the peace offerings to the inner self before those altars, brought longings and dreads in the experience of the entity—that find in the present that longing for an expression in some manner in which the application of that which has been gained may be the more individual and *not* so much national—yet national in its scope; which may be brought by the entity's application, as was done in those periods—by its writings of that which prompted those beseechings that a people be allowed to worship according to the dictates of their own conscience. For there the entity learned *tolerance,* which so few possess in *any* experience in the earth! 1298-1

Prior to her lifetime in Persia, she had been a priestess in Indochina who was influenced by the spiritual truths being promulgated in Egypt. From that experience, she had gained an appreciation of the importance of individuals finding their own spiritual truth. At the same time, however, she lost spiritually because of personal self-indulgence. During a lifetime in Atlantis, she had attempted to apply and share spiritual truths but had grown distrustful and intolerant of those who had misapplied divine knowledge. On her own part, there had been an incarnation when she had also let the material world take precedence over her spiritual purposes.

In the present, [1298] was told that she had known and experienced the rise and fall of nations because of their application and misapplication of divine truths. From those experiences, she innately knew the way to express the laws of truth in the earth. She was told to teach, to write, and to live in such a manner that others could see how "godliness" could become a practical experience in everyday life.

According to the reports on file, [1298] corresponded a number of times with Edgar Cayce and received two more readings, one of which she thought was too vague. However, in 1943, after reading the book *A Search for God,* she wrote to request additional copies and stated that she "found it priceless": "Just as my life reading cleared up so many things for me, so does this book. I am going to send one to an acquaintance in California and wish I could afford to send many, many copies to persons of my acquaintance . . . A thousand thanks for all you have done for me and mine . . . "

A follow-up reading in 1943 stated that a man she was attracted to in the present had been her betrothed during her incarnation as Esther. At that time, however, the engagement had come to an end when she had married the king instead. In spite of the attraction, [1298] remained single and never married.

Because of her past incarnations, she felt drawn to Indochina and eventually made some archaeological trips to Cambodia. During the 1950s, [1298] remained interested in the A.R.E. lecture activities that were occurring in New York. She responded to a follow-up questionnaire to her readings in 1951 and wrote that she found the information invaluable, that it had helped her better fulfill her purpose in life, and that she still referred to the information frequently:

> I have tried to help others, as Mr. Cayce suggested, open new vistas . . . whenever possible. The reading cleared up many things for me as to the continuity of life—a pattern—showed how *unimportant* one's position and how important one's life in whatever phase, newsboy or king, for growth; [it] gave me courage to keep my chin up without being

> full of self-pity and why unselfishness is so vital to one's fulfillment of the earth cycle. Each re-reading of my personal reading brings fresh inspiration . . .

She visited the A.R.E. in 1962 and a few years later published a book based on her own life readings and the readings of a few of her closest friends. In 1968, [1298] was hospitalized because of lung cancer. She was well enough, however, to appear on a television show with Hugh Lynn Cayce and Elsie Sechrist, discussing the Cayce work. The last notation on file states that she died in August 1969.

Eunice
Acts 16:1; II Timothy 1:5
Case 2138

Mother of Timothy, Eunice was a Jew who believed in her faith and later converted to Christianity. Her husband was a Greek who did not believe. Nonetheless, Eunice and her mother taught Timothy the Old Testament and gave him a firm spiritual upbringing. For that reason, Timothy became an early disciple who was much like a son to Paul. Paul would later write of the young man's faith that had been passed down from his mother and grandmother.

In 1931, a fifty-nine-year-old registered nurse was told that among her incarnations she had been Eunice:

> In the one then before this we find in that land known as the promise land, and yet the entity again a sojourner from a northern and western country. The entity then a worker in linens, and an embroiderer of no mean estate, coming in the latter period of the experience under the influence of the teacher as became the *leader,* of the chief of the *speaking*

> exponents of the new set, or sect. The entity gaining through this experience, for—as was said of the follower of Paul, "so in that graciousness of thine grandmother Eunice." The entity Eunice through this experience . . . that of the greatest faith, the greatest satisfaction, the greatest understanding; for though there be those things that would attempt to make one afraid that are of the earthly making, and those things that would bring those bindings from material things, in *Him*—as taught by Paul—*is* the light, and there *is* no variableness in His understanding. When one once gains that consciousness of that presence as was gained by the entity in that experience, nothing in the heavens above, in the seas beneath, neither far or near, can shake or change *that* understanding; for He *is* the light, and the way man *and* woman may approach the *Throne* of Grace. In the present this, as we find, brings many of those of the love of the household, yet the longing for ministering to those that are needy in any condition or position; especially love for brocades or raised figures in cloth, and for that that makes for beauty in women's apparel. 2138-1

Additional incarnations included a lifetime in New England where she had settled after experiencing religious persecution in her native country of Norway. From that period she possessed a determination to follow-through on what she believed to be right. In ancient Egypt, she had worked as a healer and still maintained the desire to influence those around her with the same spiritual truths she held within herself. Cayce told her that the line of work with which she was presently involved would best enable her to fulfill her life's mission.

That same year, she obtained a life reading for her seventeen-year-old son. For the next seven years, [2138] sent frequent notes to Edgar Cayce, often accompanied by small contributions to his work. A routine mailing to her in 1940 was returned and marked "unknown." No additional reports are on file.

Gamaliel
Acts 5:34-41, 22:3
Case 1188[2]

A great Jewish teacher, Gamaliel was known for his wisdom and for his humane interpretation of the law. The grandson of one of the judges of Israel, he led the more liberal Pharisees. He was one of the teachers of Saul of Tarsus (later Paul) and is best known for warning the Sanhedrin not to harm Peter and the other apostles by stating, " . . . if this counsel or this work be of men, it will come to naught: but if it be of God, ye cannot overthrow it . . . " (Acts 5:38-39)

Parents of a six-year-old boy obtained life and health readings for their son. During the course of the child's life reading, the parents were told that their son was extremely sympathetic to others. Apparently, on a number of occasions, the boy had been involved with laws and the interpretation of the law. In fact, in his most recent lifetime he had been John Jay, one of the leading political figures of the American Revolution and the first Chief Justice of the U.S. Supreme Court. During a lifetime in Palestine, he had also interpreted the law as a member of the Sanhedrin:

> . . . the entity proclaimed in the experience before that, as Gamaliel—one of the seventy as pre-

---

[2]In 1931, a sixteen-year-old-boy was told that he had also been named Gamaliel and had been in the same family as the Gamaliel who had petitioned the Sanhedrin on behalf of the disciples. (See 933-1.)

> sented during those experiences when the Master was in the earth and His activities were there in the temple, and during those periods when there were those distressing conditions as arose from the persecutions of those that had been His disciples or His apostles and His followers.
>
> For Gamaliel then was a teacher, yea a rabbi; but had held to that principle that if it be of God, then man had better *not* interfere, and if it is only of man's imagination and not founded in the truth it will come to naught of itself.
>
> Throughout that experience the entity gained, because of those activities and those sojourns throughout. For there was not only the individual development, but those activities or developments which gave the opportunity for others to express themselves in their relationships to their fellow men—as to that held as their ideal of their Creator, and their relationships to same. 1188-3

A previous incarnation in Chaldea had seen [1188] as a general during the time of Alexander the Great. In that lifetime he had developed an intense interest in mechanical things. In ancient Egypt, he had been a counselor to the king. The boy's reading stated that he was affectionate, sentimental, and prone to "worry over trifles." As far as his talents were concerned, he would be good at debate, but that ability might be overshadowed by his interest "in those things of a mechanical or machine nature," especially related to trains and airplanes.

According to follow-up reports, as a young man, [1188] joined R.O.T.C. and served as a lieutenant in the army. All through school and the army he maintained a deep interest in philosophy, the work of Edgar Cayce, and political science. In the 1950s he took a job with an airplane company in the Northwest. At the time, he still hoped to take a correspondence course in law. He found frequent occasions to debate philosophy and reincarnation with those of a more fundamentalist background. The last report on file is a Christmas card from 1963 when [1188] stated that he was still an employee of the same airplane company and expected to remain in the Northwest.

Haman
Esther 3-9
Case 1273

Haman is the villain in the Book of Esther and is known best for instigating one of the first campaigns against the Jews. He was the chief minister of Persia, under King Ahasuerus, and became enraged that Mordecai, a Jew, refused to bow down before him. As a result, he convinced the king to authorize a Jewish massacre. Just prior to the planned slaughter, however, Queen Esther, who had replaced Ahasuerus's deposed first wife, revealed that she too was a Jew and prevented the killing. (See also "Esther.") Afterward, Haman and his sons were hanged. This Jewish deliverance became celebrated thereafter as the feast of Purim.

In 1936, a woman received a life reading in which she was told that she had been Queen Vashti, first wife to King Ahasuerus. (See also "Vashti.") That same year, she obtained a life reading for her husband, a broker, and the two learned that they had known one another during that Persian period, for he had been Haman:

> Before that we find the entity was in the Persian land during those experiences when Xerxes or Ahasuerus was upon the throne, during those periods when turmoils arose according to the activities of Ahasuerus in the dethroning of the queen.

> The entity then was overzealous in its own personal gains, in the name then Haman, which came to be to a portion of those experiences as a byword; yet to those peoples that were in authority from what would be termed today the educational and the purposeful view, of high estate.
>
> In the material things the entity lost; again in the mental and the soul and the influences for the greater development, the entity gained.
>
> Beware in the present of the egotism of self becoming a stumblingblock. Use rather as a constructive force, and we may find not only will the material, the harmonious mental and the greater soul development arise from those associations of those experiences there, but those activities that may be as a part of the entity's sojourn or activity in the present. 1273-1

Told that he was extremely determined to do things his own way, [1273] was encouraged to learn diplomacy, interacting more gently and constructively with others. Possessing high mental abilities, he was informed that he would have a great influence over large numbers of people. He was encouraged to pursue the field of "political economics," lecturing and writing. His past lives included one during the American Revolution, where he had revolted against unfair taxation and participated in the Boston Tea Party. He had also been in Atlantis and had migrated to the Pyrenees, rising to a position of authority dealing with law and order.

He was encouraged to temper his personal beliefs and to begin showing others the same mercy he would like to receive in return. Informed that he was prompted from within by strong spiritual principles, he was assured by Cayce that he had much good to offer many people.

No personal follow-up reports are on file.

Hannah
I Samuel 1, 2
Case 1521[3]

The story of Hannah is told in the Book of Samuel. One of the two wives of Elkanah, Hannah was barren whereas her sister-wife had children. Desperate for a child of her own, Hannah prayed fervently for a son and promised that if she were given a son she would "give him unto the Lord all the days of his life." (1 Samuel 1:11) Shortly thereafter, her trust was rewarded and she became pregnant. Throughout her pregnancy she apparently kept an attitude of spiritual expectancy, and when her son was born she named him Samuel. Remembering her promise, Hannah consecrated her child's life in service to God. Samuel grew to become the first of the Hebrew prophets and a ruler of his country. Later, Hannah became the mother of five additional children and was regarded as a prophetess.

Parents of a one-week-old baby girl were told that their daughter had experienced a number of notable incarnations. In addition to having been Anne Boleyn, wife of Henry VIII, she had experienced two memorable lifetimes in the Holy Land: one as the prophetess Anna (see also "Anna") and the other as Hannah, mother to Samuel:

> Before that we find the entity was in the earth during those periods when the children of promise were in the lands of promise, when the preparations and the settlements and the changes had been wrought.

---

[3]In 1931, Cayce told a forty-one-year-old housewife (404-1) that she had also been named Hannah in a past incarnation; however, it was not the Hannah who was the mother of Samuel.

And though there were those individuals and groups who forsook the counsel of Joshua and of Moses, the entity then—as Hannah—made the overtures for that promise; and it was *that* entity [Samuel] that was *hoped,* that was visioned, that might have been a part of the experience! And yet it may be the guiding force of *this* entity through this sojourn, if there are those activities of those about the entity in the matter of the spiritual guidance that this entity may be dedicated to the spiritual laws and not material things alone.

As Hannah the entity gained throughout in those activities. And though ever looked upon by those in a material experience as one apart, one separate, the entity gained the experience of knowing that God in His heavens does take thought, does take cognizance of the prayers, of the supplications, of the activities of an individual that are in accordance with the manner and way the individual prays.

1521-1

Cayce believed that the story of Hannah was important because she lived at a time when the earth was in need of spiritual awakening—a time much like today. He encouraged the parents to obtain additional readings for [1521] when she was older.

See "Anna" for follow-up reports.

Jairus' Daughter

Matthew 9:18-26; Mark 5:21-43; Luke 8:40-56

Case 559[4]

Jairus was head of the Jewish synagogue in Capernaum

[4]In reading 421-5, a twenty-one-year-old woman was told that she also had been one of Jairus' daughters and had seen the healing of her sister by Jesus.

and came to Jesus distraught because his twelve-year-old daughter was dying. In order to be of assistance, Jesus followed Jairus to his house, healing others along the way. Unfortunately, when they arrived, Jairus was informed that his daughter was already dead. Jesus assured the crowd that she was not dead, only sleeping. He took the girl by the hand and said, "Talitha cumi," which means, "Damsel, I say unto thee arise." (Mark 5:40) Immediately, she arose and was healed.

A six-year-old girl who had previously received physical readings obtained a life reading in 1934. Cayce advised the parents that their child was extremely intelligent and possessed the ability to keep track of small details and minutia. Highly sensitive, she was also extremely intuitive. The reading warned the parents that she would be prone to a serious health problem between the ages of ten and eleven because her soul longed for the spiritual world more than it did the physical. He suggested that she be trained in music, especially with reed or string instruments. The child would also be drawn more to relationships with women than to men.

Her most recent incarnation had been in Salem, Massachusetts, during the time of the witch trials. Because she was prone to spiritual experiences, she had been seen as being different and was persecuted, although not killed. Prior to her experience in Salem, she had been alive at the time of Jesus:

> Before that we find the entity was in that land now known as Palestine, during that period when there were those that heard of and received those teachings during the experiences of the walk of the Son of man in the earth.
>
> The entity then was that one whom the Master called again from the deep sleep—Jairus' daughter. Before and after that happening, we find that the

> entity was one in the experience who gave much of self to make for the closer association and relation with the mental attributes of the spirit as related to the material things, rather than to the thoughts of material things themselves.
>
> Hence, will it be any wonder that in this sojourn, during the tender years (as then), the experience must come when more of the same influence as held the entity into the earth will be necessary in the experience, rather than those things pertaining wholly to material things? Yet, when one is in *any* environ, one is subject to the laws of same; and unless material laws are spiritualized in the mental activity of souls, those oft that are healed physically remain sick spiritually. 559-7

Prior to her lifetime in the Holy Land, [559] had been trained in Egypt as a priestess and had journeyed to the Abyssinian land (Ethiopia), becoming a spiritual leader to the people. Cayce told her that there were hieroglyphic records of that incarnation that still existed within the mountain ranges of the Upper Nile. In Atlantis she had been a loving leader who had also been responsible for services in one of the temples. In the present, the parents were encouraged to train [559] in material things that would assist her in experiencing a spiritual life, especially music and the arts.

After receiving the reading, the mother stated that she was thrilled with the information and felt that it coincided with her daughter perfectly. That same year, the child's parents separated and later divorced and [559] no longer had contact with her father. No reports indicate any unusual illness between the ages of ten and eleven. Two of her brothers were killed during World War II, and in 1948 she married a naval officer. By 1953 they had had two children.

Final reports from the 1970s state that [559] and her husband eventually had three children. She visited the A.R.E. in 1972 and requested copies of the readings that had been given to various members of her family.

Japheth
Genesis 5:32, 6-10; I Chronicles 1:4-5
Case 2627

One of the sons of Noah, Japheth is generally considered to be the eldest. Born after his father had reached the age of five hundred, Japheth and his brothers assisted the patriarch in building an ark to survive the Great Flood. Because he and his brother, Shem, covered their father's nakedness when he lay drunken in a tent after the experiment of winemaking, he and his descendents were blessed. According to Genesis, Japheth was married before the Flood and his wife accompanied him into the ark. After the Flood, the couple had seven sons. Although his wife's name is not mentioned in Genesis, Edgar Cayce stated that her name had been Rezepatha. (See also "Rezepatha.") In fact, between 1939 and 1944, various individuals were told that they had been members of Noah's immediate family. (See also "Maran," "Methuselah," "Noah," and "Shelobothe.")

In 1941, a New Hampshire dairy farmer was told that he had been Japheth:

> For, the entity was among those eight souls saved for a definite purpose, and brought that influence in the earth that is today that source from which spiritual and mental advance has been kept toward that more commonly termed the more civilized of the groups or individuals . . .
>
> For we find the entity, as the son of Noah, chose the better way for transmitting in fact, in activity, to

> his peoples after the sojourn in the ark, not only the needs for the establishing of homes but of home altars, and the uniting of those home altars in a group, a nation, a national activity.
>
> The name then was Japheth. In the experience the beauty of the companionship, of the entity's activities, not only before but after the period of preparation and throughout the sojourn, found its expression and activity in that channel through which the hope of the world did and has come again. 2627-1

Mr. [2627] was informed that his wife in this lifetime was the same wife he had been married to as Japheth. From that incarnation, he possessed the ability to rejoice and find spiritual harmony in the material world. In a recent lifetime, he had been the brother to the pirate Jean Lafitte and was encouraged to overcome some of the selfish interests that had been acquired in that period. During the reign of Caesar Augustus, he had served as a counselor, determining how the various Roman peoples might best be taxed to contribute to the empire. In Atlantis, he had been one of those who had worked with the land to produce materials upon which records might be preserved for the future.

A lover of nature, [2627] was encouraged to continue his work using the soil to supply sustenance to meet the physical needs of humankind: "In those fields of service and in the activities with the soil, with the products of the soil, with those groups that would make practical not merely by theory but by *living* practical spiritual evolution, do we find the abilities of the entity in the present." He was encouraged to use the same prayer he had often used in meditation after the Flood upon the mountain of Ararat:

"Lord, Thou art Maker of heaven and earth. Thou hast preserved Thy servant for a purpose in the earth. Thou hast given me, today, opportunities. Help me, O God, to choose the right way; that I may ever be a channel of blessings to others, pointing the way ever to Thee."

A few years later, he and his wife obtained a reading for their son [5008] and were told that the child had also been born to them as one of their first offspring after the Flood. No additional personal reports are on file.

Jason
Matthew 19:16-30; Mark 10:17-31
Case 1416

After Jesus had blessed the little children along the coast of Judaea, a young rich man came to Him and asked, " . . . what good thing shall I do, that I may have eternal life?" Jesus told him to keep the commandments, to which the young man replied that he had done just that all of his life. Jesus then encouraged him to sell all that he had and to come and join His followers. According to the Bible, the young man went away very sorrowful because he had many possessions. Although not named in the Gospels, Edgar Cayce stated that the rich young man had been called Jason.[5]

A thirty-four-year-old investor was told that throughout his life he would be inclined to travel a great deal, especially in tropical climates. Good at making and keeping friends, he was informed that he also possessed

---

[5]Gladys Davis made a notation on January 27, 1942, stating that another individual [2677] had also been told he had been the rich young man, called Nicholas in that instance: "We can only conclude that there were two, maybe more, 'rich young rulers.' Perhaps Matthew and Mark were recording different incidents of the same nature." (See also "Nicholas.")

innate talents as a physician. In his most recent incarnation he had been an employee of Benjamin Franklin's just after the American Revolution, where he had loved travel and matters of government. His reading stated that in the present he could excel in trade, commerce, or any activity that dealt with countries such as Brazil, Ceylon (now Sri Lanka), India, or Persia (Iran).

In a lifetime in the Gobi, he had been one of the ministers in authority and responsible for law and finance. In that same incarnation, he had found frequent opportunity to travel. In Atlantis, he had been among the Children of the Law of One and had made overtures of peace to the enemy, the Sons of Belial. Cayce told him that he had also been the rich young man who had asked Jesus, "How may I have eternal life?":

> Before that we find the entity during that period when the Master walked in the earth.
>
> And here we may find that question answered which has oft been asked by many in the last half century, "Who was—and what became of—the rich young ruler that came and asked 'How may I have eternal life?'"
>
> That was this entity. Hence the reason why again in the present experience the worldly goods are a portion of the entity's activities; and the abilities to distribute same as a helpful influence in the experiences of others are still a portion of the entity's activity.
>
> Much might be said as to that period of sojourn, and as to the helpful forces that came into the lives and experiences of many owing to the activities of that entity, who would be termed in the present as Jason—if the interpretation were given of the experience or name in the sojourn.
>
> The associations with those in authority, politi-

> cally, then, as the activities of the persecutions of a local nature, and those activities of the entity in inducing the Roman authorities to become a part of that deciding factor in the experiences of the earthly sojourn of many, were a part of that whole experience. 1416-1

In the present, [1416] was reminded of the importance of living so that he would, "Love the Lord with all thy heart, thy mind and thy body; thy neighbor as thyself." In 1937, he obtained a life reading for his son. The only additional file notation is from 1962 when it stated that [1416] had become a United States ambassador to Persia.

John Mark
Gospel of Mark
Case 452

According to Edgar Cayce, John Mark was born when Jesus was sixteen years old, to parents who were relatives of the Virgin Mary. Crippled from birth, he was partially healed by John the Baptist and later healed completely by Jesus. He became an associate and later a frequent companion to the apostles, Peter and Barnabas. He began to act as compiler for the two, and the letters that had been dictated to him eventually formed the basis of the Gospel of Mark. Later, he would travel with the likes of Andrew, Paul, and Luke. Though he was a prolific writer, according to Cayce many of John Mark's other materials were destroyed in the library of Alexandria. His reading stated that he was extremely helpful to members of the early Church and eventually suffered martyrdom because of his beliefs.

The mother of a twenty-seven-year-old Lutheran missionary who had served in China obtained a life reading for her son in 1932. Active in Cayce's Association, she knew that her son was not interested in topics such as reincarnation. The reading was an attempt to help her son with his life's direction. Possessing an analytical mind, [452] was told that in past experiences he had often been a seeker. One of his most influential incarnations had been as John Mark:

> In the one then before this, we find during that period when there were many turmoils among the peoples of which the entity then [was] a part. While young in years in that experience, the entity saw much of the oppressions of peoples for the thought as held, and the first account as was written by anyone (that *remains* as an account) was written by the entity under the *direction* of him to whom was given the keys of the kingdom. In the name John Mark. Be well were he to call himself John in the present! In this experience the entity suffered much in many ways, being afflicted in body and being questioned oft by superiors as one not well grounded in faith; yet the entity gained throughout the experience in the activities, in the service rendered to many. 452-1

Mr. [452] had also had an incarnation in France and had chosen to immigrate to the young United States, where he became a missionary for religious freedom. At the same time, he became involved in trade, commodities, and commerce. In Persia, he had also been involved in trade, commerce, and the exchange of ideas, working especially with China. His reading stated that some of his writings from that period still existed among the peoples of the Himalayas. In ancient Egypt, he had been a missionary, offering great service to many people of different lands. It was an experience, the reading stated, that he was destined to repeat in his present incarnation.

He was told that he could excel in directing or organizing service work for others, counseling often with missionaries and emissaries to other countries.

Because [452] received help for a physical problem, he would later request his own life reading for additional information on his incarnation as John Mark. According to file reports, he eventually became open to the topic of reincarnation and was very interested in his own life readings. No additional follow-up material is on file.

Judas Iscariot

Matthew 10:1-4, 26:14-29, 27:1-8; Mark 3:14-19, 14:10-25; Luke 6:12-16, 22:3-54; John 6:67-71, 12:1-8, 13:1-31, 18:1-13; Acts 1:16, 25

Case 5770

The only apostle not from Galilee, Judas Iscariot handled the finances for Jesus and the other apostles. The cause of his betrayal is frequently debated. Some contend that because of a zealous background, Judas was attempting to force Jesus into declaring His kingdom on earth. Regardless of the reason, after the Last Supper, he turned in Jesus to the authorities for thirty pieces of silver, pointing out his Master with a kiss. In spite of the betrayal, Jesus referred to him as "friend." When Judas Iscariot later realized what he had done, he threw the silver he had received into the temple, then committed suicide by hanging himself. Edgar Cayce confirmed that Judas Iscariot had not intended to harm Jesus because he had seen his Master evade individuals who sought to do harm many times previously.

A Jewish man very much involved in the Cayce work was told that he had been Jude, a brother to Jesus. (See also "Jude.") The man asked if his assumption were correct that a wealthy Gentile business associate he knew had been Judas Iscariot. Although the businessman in question never received a personal reading, Cayce stated that this associate had, in fact, been Judas. That individual was given case number [5770] to preserve his identity. Both the Cayce readings and the individual who had been Jude stated that Mr. [5770] was a fine man in the present (137-125).

Jude

Matthew 13:53-58; Mark 6:1-5; Epistle of Jude
Case 137

According to the New Testament, Jesus had younger brothers whose parents were also Mary and Joseph. Many contend, however, that Jesus was an only child and that when the Scriptures refer to Jesus' "brothers" they are actually meaning cousins or distant members of the same family. Edgar Cayce stated that a number of years after Jesus was born of a virgin, Mary and Joseph began normal marital relations and had several children, including a son named Jude and a daughter named Ruth. (See also "Ruth.") Apparently Jude did not believe in Jesus' claims or ministry until after the Resurrection. Later, however, he became an important member of the early Church. Well versed in the Old Testament Scriptures, he wrote the brief Epistle of Jude in the New Testament which encourages the faithful to remain firm in their beliefs in spite of those who deny the existence of the Christ.

In 1924, two brothers, Jewish stockbrokers, became an integral part of the Cayce work. For the next six-and-a-half years, they would obtain hundreds of readings, underwrite the construction of the Cayce Hospital in Virginia Beach, and explore countless topics in the readings. (See also "Elam.") Devout in their faith, they were also extremely interested in the life and teachings of Jesus. This interest was traced, in part, to the fact that the younger brother had been Jude, one of Jesus' brothers in the Holy Land: "Just before this, we find in the days when the Master came into the Promised Land. This entity one that followed close in the ways of the teachings as set by Him. In the personage of the brother in the flesh, Jude." (137-4) Cayce stated that records of Jude's writings still remained in Roman tombs that had yet to be unearthed.

Additional past lives included one in Assyria where he had served as a builder and an armorbearer to Ezekiel, and in Atlantis where he had come to know of the importance of establishing a firm spiritual foundation before attempting any endeavor. His reading stated that in the present Mr. [137] could excel in speculative occupations or in the business of construction. Also keenly interested in things of a mystical nature, he was innately intuitive and often had valid insights through waking impressions as well as in his dreams.

In spite of their involvement in the Cayce work, Mr. [137] and his brother withdrew from the Association in the early 1930s. At the time, they became involved in a small printing and greeting card company. During the same period they converted to Catholicism and joined the Catholic Church. In 1939, [137] sold his seat on the New York Stock Exchange.

In 1974, Mr. [137] visited the A.R.E. and was shown how the Association had grown. He was surprised by the magnitude of the records that had been collected. One of the final reports on file states that he died in 1980 of cancer.

Lazarus
John 11-12
Case 1924

Whenever Jesus visited Bethany, He stayed at the

home of Mary, Martha, and their brother, Lazarus. Lazarus's sudden death brought Mary and Martha much grief, and they were convinced that he could have been saved by Jesus. When news of his death reached Jesus, He wept. According to the gospel, Lazarus had been in the tomb four days when Jesus finally arrived. Upon His arrival, Jesus had the stone covering the tomb removed and commanded, "Lazarus, come forth!" Lazarus came out of the tomb, still covered in burial cloths. Jesus' raising of Lazarus from the dead caused so many of the Jews to believe that the authorities decided they needed to take drastic steps to silence Him for good. According to tradition, Lazarus eventually sailed to Marseilles with his sisters and became a bishop of the early Church. (See also "Martha" and "Mary Magdalene.")

A fifty-five-year-old naturopathic physician, consultant, and lecturer learned that he possessed innate healing abilities, capable of aiding others on both a mental and physical level. He was told that because of past-life experiences, he could gain an awareness and understanding of the application of spiritual principles in the earth that would be "surpassed by few."

In England, he had been a companion with Charlemagne, becoming adept at discerning what troubled individuals in their bodies, minds, and souls. In ancient Egypt, he became responsible for creating some of the services that were later compiled into the *Book of the Dead.* At the same time, he had served as an interpreter and an emissary for those from other lands. During an incarnation in Atlantis, he had been a ruler who had often used his intuition, sometimes for good and sometimes for material gain. From that lifetime, he had also developed an inner longing to be a "wanderer." His most notable lifetime had occurred in the Holy Land:

> In the one before this we find in that period when

> there were the many divisions in the land now known as Palestine, or the Promised Land, during that period when the Master walked in the land. The entity was then among those *to* whom the entity came, of Him, by Him, called again from the arms of that called death; being, then, the friend, the companion, of those who loved His name, who loved His manner, His way; hated of many peoples, the entity . . . In this period the entity gained throughout the experience, in the associations, in the calls that were made upon the entity—either from those in places of power or those that were oppressed by those in power, or by those who would come and seek the entity's counsel, on account of the position even occupied by the entity. Over *this* entity, and the circumstances, did even He that walked in Galilee weep. Lazarus, then, was the entity, the brother, to those whom the Lord loved. In his home, in the table, at the various functions, did the entity find the associations that have brought in the present experience those counsels, where—in places of high estate, in places of low degree, in the various sects, in the various conditions in individuals' lives—the entity has touched that which has made a change. Some are repelled; some are drawn to—yet that light, that love, as shed through that experience, brings to the entity those abilities to lay aside much that would beset many in various experiences and *give* them an understanding that is above *every* name; the abilities to heal in the hands, in the mind, in the activities—whether from within or without—is the entity blessed! 1924-1

Dr. [1924] was encouraged to remain faithful to the abilities that had been given to him and to stay true to the faith he had experienced in Palestine.

According to Gladys Davis, after the reading had been given, "Dr. [1924] spent the evening with us and held us spellbound by relating his many experiences in which he had been miraculously saved from violent death in this life. His experiences had led him to believe that no one dies until his time comes, no matter what."

Dr. [1924] was referred to the woman who had been told that she had been his sister, Mary Magdalene, in the Palestine incarnation and the two corresponded. Throughout the 1930s, Dr. [1924] and Edgar Cayce wrote one another. He also referred a number of individuals for readings. In 1946, he wrote to obtain a copy of *A Search for God* and in 1947 sent a postcard from India.

No additional reports are on file.

Lucius

Acts 13:1; Romans 16:21

Case 294

One of the leading Christians at Antioch, Lucius of Cyrene was considered a teacher in the early Church. A friend and kinsman of Paul, he was one of those involved in missionary work. According to Edgar Cayce, Lucius was also one of the seventy disciples appointed by Jesus as forerunners to prepare the way into those cities and towns to which He and His apostles planned to visit. (Luke 10:1) Later, he was chosen by John the Beloved to be bishop of the church of Laodicea. Though he was a nephew to Luke, the readings state that it was actually Lucius who wrote the Gospel of Luke.

During one of Cayce's travels in the 1930s, a number of psychics and mediums attended one of his lectures. After the program, these same individuals asked Cayce if he were aware that he had been Luke or a close associate of Luke's. Cayce brushed aside the claim, stating that nothing of such magnitude had ever been suggested by his own readings. In 1937, while giving a reading for another person, the information stated that Cayce had known the individual in Palestine when he had been Lucius of Cyrene, a relative of Luke's. Two months later, Cayce requested a reading on the identity, specifically asking why this past life had never been volunteered before. The answer was that it would have caused him to have an overinflated ego and had only been provided when he could accept it in humility.

Lucius had apparently been a soldier of fortune and a ne'er-do-well as a youth. He also maintained a relationship with a mistress even after he had married a young woman who was a member of the early Church—for a time this fact would cause him some measure of difficulty with other members of the faithful. Although he had originally felt that the mission of Jesus was to establish a kingdom on earth, after the Crucifixion and Pentecost, Lucius's witness of Peter speaking in tongues would forever change the disciple's concept of Jesus' life and vigorously recommit him to the cause:

> In those activities then that followed the Crucifixion, and the days of the Pentecost, and the sermon or teachings—and when there was beheld by Lucius the outpouring of the Holy Spirit, when Peter spoke in tongues—or as he spoke in his *own* tongue, it, the message was *heard* by those of *every* nation in their *own* tongue—this so impressed Lucius that there came a rededicating, and the determination within self to become the closer associated, the closer affiliated with the Disciples or Apostles. 294-192

The reading stated that just as Lucius had become an influence for good as well as for the rededication of individuals to a spiritual cause, Edgar Cayce could have the same influence in the present.

Additional past lives included that as a high priest in ancient Egypt, when he had also had two wives (causing him some measure of difficulty), but he primarily had been responsible for spiritual laws that had transformed that society. In ancient Persia he had been a healer and a leader who had guided a desert people into creating one of the first missionary works on earth. In Troy he had been a guard and a gifted intuitive, who was charged with defending the city through use of his psychic gift but had failed. In the eighteenth century he had been a ne'er-do-well and a trapper who had wasted his life and his psychic talent on selfish pursuits. For that reason, in the present he was to "lay self aside" every time he gave a reading.

Hundred of pages of follow-up reports are on file. Edgar Cayce died in January 1945.

Luke

Colossians 4:14; II Timothy 4:11; Philemon 24
Case 2824

Called the "physician" by St. Paul, Luke was considered a fellow worker and a companion of Paul in his travels. Early Christian tradition identifies him as the author of Acts as well as the Third Gospel—a belief contradicted by Cayce. (See also "Lucius.") He is believed to have originally been a Greek-speaking pagan before his conversion. According to tradition, he never married and lived to the age of eighty-four. The Church celebrates his feast day on October 18.

In 1942, the parents of a four-hour-old boy obtained a life reading for their son. Perhaps because of the child's age, the reading was extremely brief. In the beginning, Cayce suggested a name for their boy, [2824], based on the child's previous lives—the parents would follow the suggestion. Told that their son was very determined and would have his own way, the boy was also good-natured. His most recent past life had been as a farmer in the same ancestral family. In fact, the reading stated that the boy was the great, great grandson of himself. A careful observer of opportunities and people, according to Cayce, the boy would also be good with money. His reading advised him to become a doctor.

Additional past lives included that as an early king of Sweden. In Egypt, he had been the child of one of the Pharaohs, and in China he had been the father of his present mother. He was also known as the physician at the time of the Master. However, according to Cayce, in that life he had never finished his education nor had he ever practiced as a doctor. He had also been a writer in that experience. In the present, the boy could excel in teaching or as a physician. Perhaps because of past-life difficulties, he was advised to stay away from politics.

Follow-up reports include some correspondence from the family expressing their delight after the baby's birth. In 1951, the boy's mother requested and received an extra copy of her son's reading. While growing up, the boy's father stated that the child had been shrewd about money matters, saving money from his paper route and investing it after listening to conversations among men he respected.

In 1963, the father reported that even without knowledge of his life reading, [2824] stated that he had decided to become a doctor. He studied psychology with plans to enter medical school. However, after being made assistant to the head of the psychology department at his university, he changed his plans and obtained a doctorate in psychology.

In 1970, it was noted that he worked in educational programs for the U.S. State Department and eventually practiced as a clinical psychologist. He also taught psychology at the university level and eventually became very involved in the creation of educational programs. In 1999, friends reported that [2824] had become president of an educational research foundation.

Maran
Genesis 6-10
Case 3653

According to the Book of Genesis, Noah, his wife, his sons, and his sons' wives all entered into an ark of their own construction in order to survive the Great Flood. Although not mentioned specifically by name in the Bible, between 1939 and 1944 various individuals received life readings and were told that they had been members of Noah's immediate family. Those people included Noah's three daughters-in-law who, Cayce stated, were named Maran, Rezepatha, and Shelobothe. (See also "Japheth," "Methuselah," "Noah," "Rezepatha," and "Shelobothe.") Cayce contended that Noah's family was *one* of those who had survived the Deluge; there had been others as well. According to the Bible, after the Flood all of Noah's sons' wives had children and helped replenish the earth.

A woman who originally requested a physical reading for her father because of a magazine article she had seen about Edgar Cayce's work obtained her own life reading two months later. Given in 1944, the reading confirmed that there had been a Flood and that Noah and his family had been among those saved throughout the earth:

> For as has been given from the beginning, the deluge was not a myth (as many would have you believe) but a period when man had so belittled himself with the cares of the world, with the deceitfulness of his own knowledge and power, as to re-

> quire that there be a return to His dependence wholly—physically and mentally—upon the Creative Forces. 3653-1

The woman was told that she might be considered one of "the mothers of the world," for she had been Ham's wife and among those in the ark:

> The entity was among the peoples not of the lineage of Noah, but of those later known as the Hittites. Then the entity gave expressions to that same experience that was materially manifested in Mu, and the entity—as the wife of a son of Noah—became among the eight souls in the ark, in the preparation and in the endurance thereof, and in those experiences gained in the activities through the earth's influence.
>
> The name then was Maran. From that sojourn there is much experienced in the present in the entity's liking of the history of the early ages of man, of those experiences that are the promptings for the souls and minds of individuals, rather than the material things. 3653-1

Additional past lives included one in Lemuria, where she had been a champion for the equal rights of others and had grown spiritually and mentally. She had lived in the Holy Land during the period of the Judges and had been horrified to see a close friend of hers (Jephthah's daughter) sacrificed in fulfillment of a rash vow. She had a second incarnation in the Holy Land during the time of the prophet Mohammed, where she taught balance to others. She had also lived in the South during the time of the Civil War.

Cayce told Mrs. [3653] that she had often incarnated in the earth when there were new revelations to be made.

In the present, her talents lay in the fields of writing, teaching, and always learning new things for herself. Worried about personal finances, she was encouraged to put her labors into helping the family in ways other than financial and to keep working with things of a spiritual nature. By so doing, "the finances will follow."

Immediately after receiving the reading, she wrote: "I can't tell you how grateful I am for your help. I feel now that I'm not as useless as I have always felt, that there's something good which I can do. Every time I read your information, and I've read it many times, I find something new to think about which gives me courage. Thank you and God bless you."

No further follow-up was received for more than twenty years. Finally in 1968, she wrote and requested a copy of her reading and became a member of the A.R.E. Although she had written several songs, they had never been published. She had worked for a number of years as a teacher. Over the next six years, she wrote letters requesting information on possible publishing contacts as well as what the criteria was for utilizing case histories from the readings in books about the Edgar Cayce material.

No additional reports are on file.

Martha

Luke 10:38-42; John 11, 12:1-8

Case 560

The oldest sister of Lazarus and Mary of Bethany, Martha along with her family hosted Jesus whenever He visited Jerusalem. On one occasion, Martha was preparing food for her guests and became irritated with her sister Mary for listening to Jesus' conversation rather than helping with the dinner. At the time, Jesus reminded her that the ministry was more important than dinner. Later, when Lazarus died, Martha turned to Jesus as the only individual with whom she and her sister could find solace. According to early Church tradition, after the Crucifixion, Mary, Martha, and Lazarus journeyed by boat to Marseilles where they eventually founded a church. (See also "Lazarus" and "Mary Magdalene.")

A forty-five-year-old woman who would become very involved with the first study group and prayer group obtained a life reading. Told that the more individuals came to know her, the more she was loved, [560] held firm to friendships. Her reading mentioned that she had a strong intellect as well as the capacity to see beyond the normal understanding of others. In this respect she was a visionary, of other people and philosophies. In terms of her own growth, her past lives had caused her to possess a great deal of innate fear that needed to be overcome in the present.

In her most recent life, Miss [560] had been a frontierswoman in Virginia and had lost her life relatively early when a cave which she was exploring collapsed upon her. She had also been in England and was a member of the royal family when Charles I was beheaded. At the time, she had aided Charles II in his escape to France and had learned to maintain her faith even in the face of physical oppression. She had also experienced an incarnation at the time of Jesus:

> In the one before this we find in that land now known as the promised land, and during that period when there were the walkings in the land of the Promised One. The entity among those that were close *to* the Master, being then the sister to one of those that the Master raised from the dead [Lazarus] living in Bethany in that experience. Hence those of that period are near and dear, and far *from* those things that hinder from *knowing* of those that would

> separate the entity from those experiences! Gaining, sure, through the experience, and giving much to many; though called by those that in the experience would bring censure for the parts chosen [as Martha], or those of the secular things of life, yet in the present—with the experience—brings that *practicability* of the entity, that in groups, in associations, has ever been called—while the dreamer, yet all *practical* thought must be in accord *with* the life lived, with the circumstances as surround, with the conditions in which people find themselves—*these* are the better part, as was in that experience . . . The one, the sister to Mary—Martha. 560-1

In her present life, she was encouraged to learn to express that same love in service toward others that she had manifested as Martha.

Miss [560] also learned that she had been in ancient Persia, a member of the leader's household. At the time she had begun to hold grudges toward others, but it was a shortcoming that had been greatly overcome because of her activities in other incarnations. In ancient Egypt, she had been active in one of the temples and had learned to be of service to those who sought spiritual understanding and mental enlightenment. That incarnation provided her in the present with an interest in spiritual healing and prayer.

Miss [560] became very active in the prayer group started in 1931 and served as the group secretary. Extremely interested in meditation and prayer, she sought how the group could become of greater service to others. In 1938 she was diagnosed with breast cancer and died in January 1939 at the age of fifty-two. According to the notations on file, her presence was greatly missed by all those involved in the group activities of the Association.

Mary Magdalene

Matthew 27:56-61, 28:1-9; Mark 15:40-47, 16:1-11; Luke 7:36-50, 8:2, 10:39-42, 24:1-11; John 11:1-45, 12:1-8, 19:25, 20:1-18

Case 295

Most Church scholars state that Mary of Bethany and Mary Magdalene were two different individuals; however, Edgar Cayce contends that they were one and the same and that Mary Magdalene was the sister of Lazarus and Martha. (See also "Lazarus" and "Martha.") He stated that there had also been *two* incidents where a woman taken in adultery was about to be stoned (John 8:1-12), one of whom was Mary Magdalene. At the time, Jesus said that whoever was without sin could cast the first stone. He then stooped down and wrote upon the ground, enabling the woman's accusers to see their own sins written in the sand.

According to the Bible, Jesus healed Mary Magdalene of seven "demons," which suggest physical, emotional, and moral problems. After her healing, she became one of the holy women who supported Jesus and His disciples and accompanied them on some of their travels. A witness to the Crucifixion, she journeyed to the tomb with a woman known as "the other Mary" to anoint Jesus' body with herbs. (See also "Mary, the Other.") An angel who met the two told them that Jesus had risen. As Mary Magdalene journeyed to tell the apostles what she had seen, Jesus presented Himself.

A single, twenty-six-year-old secretary was advised in 1929 that because of past-life experiences she would innately be prone to affairs of the heart as well as to unhappiness in marriage. In her most recent life, she had been a daughter of Louis XVI of France and the only member of the royal family to escape to safety. In that incarnation, she had fled to Austria, learned to become of service to others, and had also worked as a singer. Previous to that, she had lived at the time of Alfred the Great in England. Prone to self-condemnation in the present, the woman was told that her most notable life had been as Mary Magdalene:

> In the one before this we find in that period when the Master walked among men. To her the Master said, "She hath chosen the better part." [Luke 10:42] In ministering to Him through that period, loved by Him in that experience, as the *sister* of Martha and of Lazarus, the entity gained through the experience—and little is the wonder to others that ever the song, or the wish, or the desire for help and succor and aid is paramount in the *entity's* soul; for only that others *might* be aided did the entity enter into another experience—for, as was said by Him: "Wherever my gospel is preached, her works will be spoken of" [Matt. 26:13]. What a heritage! In the present experience we find that His tenets, His truths, are easily taught, understood by the entity. Only be broader in the vision, condemning none—even as He condemned not even those who persecuted Him. Condemnation in the entity is *builded.* Blot *this* from *thine* experience, *through* Him who maketh all things possible. 295-1

Prior to her incarnation as Mary, she had lived in ancient Egypt and had served as a counselor and a musician. In Atlantis, she had been a princess, gaining a love of pomp and self-importance, but had also served as a healer. In the present, her talents lay in the fields of statistics, spiritual healing, and music.

Later, Miss [295] requested and received additional information on her life as Mary Magdalene:

In giving a detailed account of the experience as Mary, the sister of Martha and Lazarus, indeed much might be given respecting the activities of the entity in that experience. For, as given in the Gospel account, this entity was then the Mary of Magdalene; or the courtesan that was active in the experiences both of those that were in the capacity of the Roman officers, Roman peoples, and those that were of the native lands and country.

When the body met first the Master, it was the woman brought before the council as taken in adultery; and the one whom the whole council or court at the time asked that, according to the law, the woman be stoned.

With the cleansing of the body-mind, through the association and experience, the entity then joined again with those of the family from whom she had been separated in Bethany, and became then again of the household of those that dwelt there.

Hence the showing in the Gospel of the difference in attitude, in the manner of approach, with the various visits of the Master through the period.

The entity was the same to whom the Master first appeared upon the resurrection morn; the same to whom many of the apostles and leaders during that experience went for counsel, in the ways and manners that are spoken of in the various accounts that are kept in the present.

As to the experiences before meeting the Master, these were more of the worldly nature; wherein there was the giving of self in body, in the indulgencies of the period, such that there was brought for the body and those associated with same the activities that brought condemnation, as well as the pomp, the power, the splendor, when considered from that

> angle, in the experience of the entity through the period . . .
>
> With the death and separation of the Master from the disciples (as it may be called), the home of Mary and Martha became—for the time—rather the center from which most of the activities of the disciples took place, who were of that activity; that is, who were not altogether Galileans, see? 295-8

For a number of years, Miss [295] was very active in the first study group as well as the Glad Helpers Healing Prayer Group. In 1931, she wondered about following a boyfriend out West to marry him, but changed her mind. In 1934 she reported:

> I have felt very strongly about marriage since I have been old enough to reason (by the way, if the skeleton in the closet is in the past, it must be the divorce of my parents and the subsequent remarriages of my mother) for I have been very averse to marriage and a man-hater—can you feature that? until recently, or, I would say, until the last few years. My home conditions were very unhappy, never having had a normal home life, and I had figured out that marriage brought on all the unhappiness and misery there was in the world. Of course, I know this is all wrong now (also I had the wrong presentation of life and what it was all about when quite young), but it is hard to uproot when it is so deeply imbedded . . .

In 1935, she left Virginia for personal reasons (she had became enamored with a married man) and to help her invalid mother in Oklahoma. She later wrote to the A.R.E.: "While it wrung my heart to leave the work there (how much you will never know), I had to make the sacrifice . . ." She finally married in 1938 and had her first baby in 1940. She also worked for the telephone company for many years.

According to family and friends, she and her husband fought all the time. In 1945, [295] wrote, "Neither of us has been very happy in our marriage." By that time, the couple had two daughters. In 1961, she reported that she and her husband were still together, that both of her daughters were getting a college education, and that one daughter had married. A report from 1964 states, "My life reading helped me to understand myself and be able to overcome condemnation. I really feel that if I hadn't learned what I did through Edgar Cayce's readings, I would have remained an old maid . . ."

In 1968, she reported that she had retired from the phone company and now had the opportunity to travel. A grandmother, she was active in both Sunday school and church work. She and her husband eventually healed their relationship; in 1973 she wrote that they were about to celebrate their thirty-fifth wedding anniversary. In the early 1970s, her husband became ill with lymphosarcoma. After he died in 1975, she wrote, "I miss him so!" Active in A.R.E. and her church until her own death, [295] passed away in November 1987.

Mary, the Other

Matthew 27:56-61, 28:1-9;
Mark 15:40-47, 16:1-8; Luke 24:1-11
Case 2946

According to scholars, "the other Mary" referred to in Scripture is most likely the same individual as Mary the mother of James and Joses (Joseph). What is known is that "the other Mary" was one of the holy women and present at the Crucifixion. She also journeyed to the tomb with Mary Magdalene to anoint Jesus' body with herbs. (See also "Mary Magdalene.")

According to Edgar Cayce, "the other Mary" had been one of the Essene children raised as potential channels for the birth of the Christ child. Later, she was the woman at whose wedding Jesus turned water into wine. (John 2:1-11)

A writer, speaker, and former missionary to China received a life reading in 1943. Researching Edgar Cayce's psychic ability for a national magazine, she eventually wrote a popular article about his work. Her reading told her that although her past-life experiences might not be considered always "beautiful," her soul had constantly grown in the process. Depending upon her application of her abilities in the present, she had the potential to become very wealthy. Regardless of the outcome, however, she would always have sufficient for her needs.

Interested in beauty, harmony, and in concise judgments, [2946] was told that her past lives included that of a miner's wife who had traveled throughout Missouri, Colorado, and Nevada. From that experience she had gained a love of home and family as well as a tendency to want to roam. In a past life in China, she had been a princess with a great love of her people, who had striven to share the knowledge of one God with her subjects. In ancient Egypt, she had been one who had held to spiritual tenets and beliefs even in the midst of a great rebellion. In that incarnation she had served as a teacher, a speaker, and a writer. She had also been "the other Mary" at the time of Jesus:

> For, the entity was among those of the household that entertained the Master oft; then being an aid to "Mrs. Zebedee," as would be ordinarily termed. John and James were charges or cares of the entity during that experience, and the entity was among those spoken of and referred to as "the other Mary,"

> when no other indication is given as to the place from which the entity came, or as to the group to which the entity belonged.
>
> These brought the entity close in contact with the holy women. Especially during those periods following the Crucifixion, the entity became acquainted the better with the Mother. For, as the Mother became a part of that care, that charge of John, the associations became close. 2946-2

Later, Mrs. [2946] would obtain additional information on her Palestine incarnation:

> We find that the entity was among those of the group selected as channels considered worthy for the incoming of the promise of God with man.
>
> Thus the entity from its early experience was dedicated to a service to the promises which had been made from the days of the mother of men, until Malachi; that the great, the dreadful day of the Lord would be at hand.
>
> The entity, then, was that one at whose wedding the water was turned to wine, as the bride of the brother of James and John, the sons of Zebedee—Roael, as the individual entity, the elder of the children of Zebedee, a zealot for those principles of the law.
>
> Thus, with those activities that brought about the questionings because of John the Baptist making those charges against those in political authority, the husband of the entity was among those that suffered persecution and death.
>
> Hence we find that hate of war, in the experiences, the desire to quell mob, to quell those things that would cause rancor of any nature in the hearts of men.

> These, as we shall see in others, became a part of the experience of the entity.
>
> Thus the close association of the entity in the household of Zebedee. For, especially John, the younger of those chosen, that one beloved of the Master, was as a favorite of the entity, with the sorrows that had come—even though the faith, the doubtings had been indicated in the blessings of having the Master present at the wedding. 2946-3

In the present, Cayce told [2946] that her work with speaking would decrease at the same time her writing increased. She was encouraged to write fiction as well as books on popular psychology. She obtained a number of additional readings and her son eventually became very involved with Cayce's Association. She died in February 1977 of cancer, after a short illness. No additional information about her writing pursuits is on file.

Matthew

(also known as Levi)
Matthew 9:9-13, 10:1-4; Mark 2:13-17, 3:14-19;
Luke 5:27-32, 6:13-16; Acts 1:12-14
Case 417

Originally named Levi, Matthew was a dishonest tax collector who was called by Jesus to be one of His apostles. The scribes and Pharisees could not understand how Jesus could associate with such an individual. Trained as a careful record keeper, Matthew is believed to have been the author of the First Gospel, preserving many of Jesus' sayings, including the Sermon on the Mount. Tradition states that he served as a missionary in Judea, Ethiopia, Persia, and Parthia and was eventually martyred.

A thirty-five-year-old Hebrew clothier obtained a life reading and was told that he was influenced at a soul level by reason, love, beauty, honor, and justice. His reading advised him that his greatest satisfaction could be found by following the teachings of love and service promulgated by Jesus, for he had once been a close companion:

> In the one before this we find in that period when there were changes in the land of promise, and the entity was called by the Master, in the place of collector of custom, and much has been given to the world through the attempt of the entity to explain the position of his *peoples* to the Master. The entity then was in the name Matthew. In this experience the entity gained. Gained through the association, through the intent and purport, through the desire to set *others* aright. In the present we find that innate which is truth *to* the entity, that the entity desires to give to another in the *manner* as received by self. 417-1

Additional lives included an English incarnation where Mr. [417] had been responsible for providing clothing and bodily adornments to royalty. In ancient Egypt he had been one of the keepers of the household for a high priest and had gained in his ability to serve, but had lost in his attempt to control others through power. In India he had been a merchant trader, involved in the exchange of commodities such as silks, embroidery, gold, and precious stones.

In the present, [417] was encouraged to continue his work in any line that enabled him to barter and sell. He was also advised to live a well-rounded life, grounded in love and spiritual principles. If he lived in such a manner, he was destined to acquire much both spiritually and materially. Quick to speak, he was told to learn to think twice before speaking.

According to reports on file, over the next few years

[417] referred more than a dozen people to Edgar Cayce for readings of their own. In 1950, it was reported that he had become involved with the restaurant business. The last notation on file states that Mr. [417] and his wife had retired, were living in Florida, and had attended a lecture by Hugh Lynn Cayce in 1962 when Hugh Lynn was in their area.

Methuselah
(also known as Methusael or Methushael)
Genesis 4:18, 5:21-27; I Chronicles 1:3
Case 1851

According to Scripture, Methuselah lived to be 969 years old, longer than any other individual in the Bible. One of the patriarchs of humankind, he was the father of Lamech and therefore the grandfather of Noah. (See also "Noah.")

In 1939, a sixty-five-year-old brain specialist who received a life reading was told that he had been the "eighth from Adam":

> For the entity was the eighth from Adam [see Gladys Davis's note[6]], and in the days of the exodus and the periods of understanding through those activities; journeying more from what is now the Chaldean than the Egyptian land, though spending many of the periods in the activities through which the records were set as for things that were, that were to be—these became a part of the study of the entity throughout those periods.

---

[6]Gladys Davis's note: "In Mr. Cayce's Bible group I heard him refer many times to Enoch as the 'seventh from Adam,' who walked with God and was not because God took him. If this is true, then Methuselah would be the 'eighth from Adam.'"

> Hence oft the entity may lose self in those things that are found there. For, as that was the interpreting of the earth as it was, as it is, as it is to be, so came those activities to preserve same for the seeker to know his relationships to the past, the present and the future, when counted from the material standpoint.
>
> And as the entity sought in those experiences to make time and space, as well as patience, the realms that express the universality of the Force called God, so may *this* become in the present experience that in which the entity may excel—in giving that assurance to those who seek their closer understanding of the relationships one to another.
>
> 1851-1

In England, Dr. [1851] had been a priest and a "light bearer" to those around him, often explaining the relationship of all of creation to the Creator. He had been an Essene in the Promised Land during the time of Jesus and had heard the Master speak. From that experience he possessed the ability to be at peace and to share his love of nature and his love of beauty with others. In ancient Persia, [1851] had served the people as a counselor and as an interpreter of visions, dreams, and the stars. In the present, Dr. [1851] was told that he still possessed the capacity to be a torch bearer to others, bringing them hope, faith, and spiritual understanding.

According to a notation by Gladys Davis, he was still active as a physician in 1962 at the age of eighty-nine. The last report on file is from 1974 when his niece visited A.R.E. and stated that her uncle had died a few years previously.

Miriam

Exodus 2:1-10, 15:19-22; Numbers 12:1-15, 20:1, 26:59; Deuteronomy 24:8-9; I Chronicles 6:3; Micah 6:4
Case 1919

Sister of Moses and Aaron, Miriam reportedly watched her baby brother be set adrift in a cask upon the Nile in order to escape Pharaoh's decree that all Hebrew male children were to be killed. (See also "Abatha.") When Pharaoh's daughter discovered the infant, Miriam offered to find a nursemaid to feed her brother Moses. The request was granted, and she returned with her own mother. Later, after the Israelites had been freed from Egypt and crossed the Red Sea, Miriam led the women in a song of triumph. Although a prophetess and a leader of her people, she spoke out against Moses for an interracial marriage to an Ethiopian woman. Because of her indiscretion, she was stricken with leprosy but was quickly healed by Moses himself. Since she was held in such high esteem by the Israelites, a form of her name "Mary" was thereafter given to many Jewish girls.

A fifty-one-year-old Protestant housewife, who had been born in Germany, received a life reading in 1931. It stated that she was skilled at creating a home and that love and graciousness were two of the greatest influences in her life. She was also a loving companion and an excellent neighbor. In terms of her spiritual growth, the reading suggested that she claimed very little about herself but had actually applied a great deal.

In terms of her past lives, she had been born to early settlers in Quebec. From that experience she possessed a longing to always apply spiritual ideals even in the face of new situations. In an earlier incarnation in (what is now) Germany, she gained in her service of those who defended the country, but lost because of her hatred for those who attacked it. From that experience she also championed freedom of speech and personal liberties. Prior to that, she had been Miriam:

> In the one before this we find in that period when there were the transitions or changing of the peoples from the land now known as Egypt. The entity was then among those of the household of Ephraim, and returned with those peoples through the lands; gaining in the application of self, becoming—in the latter days—those peoples from whom the leader sprang as the only woman judge in Israel. The entity was then in the name Miriam. In the present, the abilities to plan, build, for those who would come later, innate and manifested in the entity's expression of that held, whether as religious tenets, moral codes, or of the aptitudes in the laws of *whatever* land the entity may be an inhabitant. 1919-2

In the present, [1919] was encouraged to assist others in creating and building their homes. She possessed an ever-living source of faith that she was advised to share with those around her. When asked about assisting her daughter in buying and building a home, she was given every encouragement by the reading. A couple of months later, Mrs. [1919]'s husband suffered a breakdown from stress, and the couple journeyed to California for an extended period of recuperation. She noted that they were still a happy couple in all other respects and had just celebrated their silver anniversary. No additional follow-up reports are on file.

Nadab

Exodus 6:23, 24:1-11, 28:1;
Leviticus 10:1-3; Numbers 3:2-4, 26:60-61;
I Chronicles 6:3, 24:1-2
Case 257

Nadab was the eldest son of Aaron and Elisheba. A leader of the children of Israel, he was one of the few permitted to be with Moses on Mount Sinai. Unfortunately, in spite of the fact that they were told not to do it, he and his brother, Abihu, created a "strange fire" on the day of their consecration into the priesthood which ended up consuming them both.

A lifelong friend of Edgar Cayce's, Mr. [257], received his first life reading in 1923 at the age of thirty and a follow-up life reading in 1926. Throughout the course of his life, [257] would obtain over two hundred readings on such topics as business advice, health, and relationships. A Jewish businessman and furniture manufacturer, he referred hundreds of individuals to Edgar Cayce for readings of their own.

According to his reading, Mr. [257] would excel in business in terms of textiles or in the manufacture of products that utilized the earth's resources. A lover of home and family, he possessed a great deal of personal integrity and a desire for truth. Because of past-life experiences, he was drawn to the mysteries of life and things of a spiritual nature. He was destined to have much in terms of worldly goods. Extremely persistent, talkative, and good-natured, he was warned to take care of his physical body because of detrimental forces that could manifest at the age of forty-eight or forty-nine.

During the American Revolution he was an aide to General Howe and had gained abilities as a leader and a supervisor. (In the present, [257] served as a captain during World War I.) In Germany, he had risen from being a farm laborer to a leader of his people in helping to put down invasions from those who hoped to conquer the land along the Rhine. From that experience he gained the ability to make speeches and to inspire others. He had been along the seashore during the time of Jesus and had witnessed some of the Master's works firsthand. He served as an assistant to Ezekiel and helped to rebuild the walls of the Holy City. Another incarnation in Palestine had been as Nadab:

> Before this the entity was in the land where the peoples were become the separate and distinct people, and was of the priesthood of that people, and in that time was he one of those offering strange fire upon the altar [Nadab]. 257-5

Additional past lives had included that as a defender of a high priest in Egypt and in Atlantis during the time of the thought forms.

Mr. [257] was reminded that service to others was the highest service to God. He was encouraged to stay in business or sales for himself and to focus on commodities or manufacturing, assisting others through his line of work.

Because of [257]'s lifelong connection and friendship with Edgar Cayce, literally hundreds of pages of notations and follow-up reports are on file. Throughout his life, he obtained countless business readings and advice on his work, his employees, his business associates, and his plans for the future. A report in 1924 states that he was sometimes making between $10,000 and $20,000 every two months in commissions. When he fell in love with a New York stage actress, he sought a reading on the advisability of getting married to her and, with Cayce's approval, married her in 1927. The couple would later obtain joint readings for themselves as well as readings for their two sons.

Although financially successful, he once told several friends that he had lost out on $500,000 dollars by not following some of Cayce's business advice in the readings. In his late forties, [257] was diagnosed with cancer but managed to live until the age of seventy-four. Even after Cayce's death in 1945, he and his wife remained lifelong supporters of the Cayce work, frequently sponsoring activities and lectures for the Association. Confirming inclinations given in his children's readings, his eldest son would become a leading psychiatrist and his youngest a successful attorney. He passed away in 1968.

Naomi
Book of Ruth
Case 1923

Due to famine, Naomi, her husband, and their two sons left Bethlehem and journeyed to Moab in search of a better life. Eventually her husband died and her two sons married. After ten years, however, her two sons died as well, causing Naomi to decide to return to Bethlehem. She tried to convince her daughters-in-law, Orpah and Ruth, to return to their own families, but Ruth insisted on accompanying Naomi. (See also "Ruth.") Because Naomi had so changed in appearance over the years because of poverty and the hardships she had experienced, her family and neighbors in Bethlehem no longer recognized her. She stated that instead of Naomi (which means "pleasant") she wished to be called Mara ("bitter"). After Ruth married Boaz, Naomi's relative, Naomi became nursemaid to their child. (See also "Boaz.")

Parents of a seven-week-old baby girl obtained a life reading for their daughter. Advised that the girl possessed a strong temper and will, they were also told that she would be one with whom they could reason. Since she would be extremely intuitive, they were encouraged not to make fun of their daughter's imagination. Throughout life, the daughter would immediately express her desires and needs and would be outgoing in ways that could be beneficial to others. The child was also a lover of rhyme and colors and possessed the ability to see the manifestation of spirit in all things.

She had lived during the early founding of the United States and had been persecuted for her beliefs and her intuitive visions. In spite of the persecution, her intuition had continued to develop, even though she died at a very young age. In France, she had also been persecuted for her beliefs and for her political associations. From that same experience she had also acquired a love of show and dress and bodily adornments. Just prior to that, she had been in the Holy Land:

> In the one before this we find in that period when there were those peoples in the land of promise, and when the peoples of the *beliefs* of the entity were persecuted by those in power; yet being in possession of those abilities to shut the conscious self out, allowing forces of the soul's development to manifest, even the first king of Israel came *to* the entity for counsel. Then in the name Naomi. The entity gained and lost through this experience, for many of the acts were evil spoken of through the *manner* in which the entity *used* same for *self's* own interests. In the present we will find the entity will be tending to hide many of those associations, unless openness, frankness, and such, are drilled and taught *to* the entity in no uncertain manner. 1923-1

In Egypt, [1923] had been one of the chiefs in the temple and had gained leadership abilities as well as a love for music.

The parents were told that, depending on their daughter's

upbringing, their child could be of great service to many people. Her intuitive abilities could be a source of guidance for herself and for others. Immediately after receiving the reading, her father wrote: "We are going to follow out the suggestions given in the life reading for our baby."

No additional follow-up reports are on file.

Nehemiah
Ezra 2:2; Book of Nehemiah
Case 1767

Nehemiah was known for his leadership and his determination to inspire the Jews to rebuild the walls of Jerusalem. While in Babylon, after hearing of the poor condition of his people in Palestine, he obtained permission to go to Jerusalem and assist in the rebuilding of the walls. When he arrived, Nehemiah united a discouraged and apathetic people who had failed repeatedly in their attempts to rebuild the city. Under his leadership, the walls finally rose from nothing but charred rubble. Later, after he returned to Babylon, he went to Jerusalem to help clean up some of the abuses and moral decline that had occurred within the community. He supported Ezra, the leader-priest-scribe, in the strict measures laid down to preserve the Jewish way of life. He is the author of the Old Testament book that bears his name.

In 1939, a wealthy American industrialist obtained a life reading. A seventy-six-year-old Catholic, he had been unable to obtain a divorce from his wife and had lived for years with his girlfriend, a woman twenty years his junior. His reading told him that he was very determined and therefore able to accomplish whatever his mind set itself upon. Democratic in his ideas, he was a champion of freedom of thought, activity, and choice. Tenderhearted and interested in things of a spiritual nature, he did not hesitate to give credit to those around him. His reading stated that romance was extremely important to him and needed to be a part of his everyday experience.

His most recent life had been during the settling of the United States, when he had been a dreamer and a visionary about possibilities and achievements. Because he had not been able to achieve at that time, he had brought that desire with him into the present. One of his most influential lives occurred in Rome during the time of Constantine. He had witnessed a large measure of conflict between the leaders of the Church and those in political authority. As a result, he had acquired a deep desire to reconcile the ideas of church and state, becoming a champion of freedom for all. He had also lived during the time of the Old Testament:

> Before that we find the entity was again in the activities of the builder, when there was the second and third return of the people of promise from the lands where they had been in exile for so long.
>
> There we find the entity was the leader, the lawyer, the soldier, the director—Nehemiah.
>
> And if there will be the perusal of those things that are considered as the messages of Ezra, as well as those of the activities accredited to Nehemiah, we may find much that is responding to something within as to the desires and purposes of the entity even in the present experience.
>
> The abilities as the builder, the abilities as to judge, as to the thought and as to the ability of producers in *any* field of service.
>
> And as the entity then sought to give example to those over which the entity had authority, those who were willing to work, those who would work must be willing to work for the purpose and to work

> with and never *for* the entity or the individual, but work with towards the building of something within the mind, the heart, the soul of each entity for the *greater* purpose for which each soul finds expression in materiality! 1767-2

In ancient Egypt, he had served as a counselor to the Pharaoh during a period of rebellion. At the time, he had been able to unify various opinions related to political, social, and religious matters.

Because of his past incarnations, [1767] possessed innate abilities as a leader and a counselor, being able to listen to those around him. In Atlantis, he had been a follower of the children of the Law of One and had frequently counseled how every individual was dependent upon all others. In that incarnation, his present girlfriend had been his mother.

In the present, he was encouraged to use his resources and abilities to bring to others an awareness of their relationship to the Creative Forces. He was also counseled to remember that truth needed no justification, but to simply be lived as an example to others.

According to reports on file, in 1939 his girlfriend requested a physical reading for him for a heart problem. One of the few reports on file is from 1952, after he had died, when his girlfriend submitted a follow-up report about the accuracy of [1767]'s reading. She confirmed all that his reading had stated, including that he was able to accomplish whatever he set out to do, that he was tenderhearted with everyone around him, that he was romantic, and was a champion of freedom of thought.

No additional reports are on file.

Nicholas
Matthew 19:16-30; Mark 10:17-31
Case 2677

After Jesus blessed the little children along the coast of Judaea, a young rich man came to Him and asked, " . . . what good thing shall I do, that I may have eternal life?" Jesus told him to keep the commandments, to which the young man replied that he had done just that all of his life. Jesus then encouraged him to sell all that he had and to come and join His followers. According to the Bible, the young man went away very sorrowful because he had many possessions. Although not named in the Gospels, Edgar Cayce stated that the rich young man had been called Nicholas.[7]

In 1942, a twenty-one-year-old prelaw university student received a life reading and was told that an innate character trait was his desire to know the "whys" and reasons for things. He was prone to set stringent boundaries for his own conduct and to be rather stern in his judgments. A lover of history who possessed a mathematical mind, he was also deeply interested in music, art, harmony, and the mechanics of music.

Told that his past lives had been quite varied, he had been among the colonists in Philadelphia during the American Revolution, carrying some measure of influence with those who drafted and approved the Declaration of Independence. He also had a rather remarkable incarnation during the time of Jesus:

> And the entity was among those—yea, that one

---

[7]Gladys Davis made a notation on January 27, 1942, stating that two individuals had been told they had been the rich young man, one called Nicholas and another named Jason: "We can only conclude that there were two, maybe more, 'rich young rulers.' Perhaps Matthew and Mark were recording different incidents of the same nature." (See also "Jason.")

about whom much speculation has been in the minds of many, over what is written there in the records, concerning which many a verbose orator has proclaimed much about which he knew so little. For, the entity was the rich young ruler who declared, "These have I kept from my youth up. What lack I yet?" "Sell that thou hast, come and follow me." "And he went away sorrowing."

But remember another line, "The Master loved the young man."

He whom the Master has favored, in mind or in purpose, may count his soul indeed fortunate. Remember one of those eternal laws, "He hath not willed that any soul should perish."

The entity then was in the name Nicholas, and the entity did just that—he came, later, and followed. Who prompted Nicodemus to seek the Lord? Who prompted those that cared for the body when it was placed in a new tomb yet unused?

These are the sources of that which is the greater virtue of the entity in the present—tolerance. This is the basis for patience, and in patience—my son—even as He gave, ye become aware of thy soul and its relationships to the purposes of infinity with the finite, and the ways of man seeking—seeking oft his own undoing, through the gratifying of the flesh and the glory of the own ego!

Then, these be channels—yea, facts—that may sink into thy consciousness. And the oft reading of same may bring oft the answer to those problems that will arise in thine experience between individuals, groups, corporations even, that seek to conform to judgments pronounced even by others in the finite manner of self-preservation.

In thy understandings, hold fast to that as ye gained through that experience. For, the entity then

> was a student of the law, which meant a student of the unwritten as well as that interpreted from the penal, the spiritual and the marital code. And these will be portions of thy experience in this sojourn.
>
> Much of thy ability, of thy understanding, applied in the study of these precepts—yea, of these concepts of His, the Master's judgments in that experience, will be needed in this world of turmoil—as man begins to learn, "I am indeed my brother's keeper."
>
> For, thou may indeed aid in bringing His day to pass. Shun not the privilege that will be thine.
>
> 2677-1

Mr. [2677] had also been a Greek, involved with the law and with discovering ways of bringing material welfare to others. In that lifetime, he eventually immigrated to Persia, becoming personally involved with healing and ministering to others. In Atlantis he had been a mathematician and an engineer.

In the present, he was advised that he could use his abilities in law. He was encouraged to discover ways to unite individuals and nations rather than separate them. A good conversationalist, he excelled in communications and would be happiest in everyday life as long as he could exercise his spiritual principles.

The first report on file is from [2677]'s mother who stated that her son had said that the reading made a great impression on him. The young man had written to his mother, "I am astounded at Mr. Cayce's reading, if for nothing else because he was so able to pick out the problems that confront me, problems that I really never put into words, even in my own thoughts." He later wrote the Cayces, "It seems impossible that those six pages could have so much power. For the first time I can see that there is a deep purpose in [our] existence, that we have a goal, not only as an idealist, but as a factualist. That this new knowledge I have is even more true than all I knew before . . . Once in a while, when I find myself being intolerant or a little impatient, the thought of the reading is enough to erase all the feeling that is negative."

In 1942, [2677] was called into the army. The next year his mother wrote a fiction story based upon her son's past life as Nicholas for the *A.R.E. Bulletin*. While at school he wrote Mr. Cayce about his girlfriend whom he hoped to marry. He also commented upon how much he enjoyed the Cayce biography, *There Is a River*, and shared it with some of his friends.

In 1950, [2677] took his bar exam; by 1953 he was a prosecuting attorney in California. The last report on file states that he did marry the girlfriend he had asked about when in college, and by 1958 they had three children.

Nicodemus
John 3:1-21, 7:43-53, 19:38-42
Case 3021

A man of wealth, Nicodemus was a member of the Jewish Sanhedrin. A prominent Pharisee, he was known to visit Jesus in secrecy, causing some to believe that Nicodemus was an ardent (if secretive) disciple. He also pleaded for Jesus' just treatment by the courts when Jesus had been arrested. After the Crucifixion, Nicodemus provided aloe and myrrh for the burial.

In 1943, a forty-four-year-old man received an emergency physical reading because he suffered from the "final stages of hypertension." His eyesight was fading, he had lost a kidney, and the doctors were fearful of hemorrhages. The reading acknowledged the serious condition, but affirmed that the problem need not be fatal. Suggested therapies included injections of vitamins, massage, physical adjustments, and dietary recommendations. Unfortunately, Mr. [3021] contracted pleurisy and pneumonia within a few weeks and was unable to keep down food. His wife notified the Cayces of her husband's passing: "On June 13 my beloved husband, [3021], passed from this life into the next, and I am experiencing the great loneliness and heartache that comes to those whose loved one has gone ahead. I want to thank you most sincerely for your help, your prayers, and your understanding sympathy."

A month later, his widow obtained a life reading and wanted to know when she and her late husband had been together previously. The reading told her that they had been together as brother and sister during the colonial period, in Egypt as rivals, and in the Holy Land as husband and wife at a time when her husband had been Nicodemus and she had been a woman named Martha, sister of Peter's mother-in-law and a member of the Essene community. Later, additional information was obtained on that Holy Land experience:

> Then there came those great changes in the life experience of Martha. For one among those of the rulers of the synagogue sought the entity in marriage and through the individuals who made these arrangements the entity was espoused to Nicodemus. Through his activities, and personality, Martha learned first of what had happened to the peoples in the homes of John the Baptist and of Mary and Joseph and Jesus.
>
> Thus, when there were later the experiences of those entering into activities, and then when the message was given out that Martha's older sister had been healed from a terrible fever by this man, Jesus, this brought about great changes in Nicodemus and Martha, as they had to do with the temple and

> the service of the high priest. Martha began the weaving of the robe that became as a part of the equipment the Master had. Thus the robe was made especially for the Master. In color it was not as the robe of the priest, but woven in the one piece with the hole in the top through which the head was to be placed, and then over the body, so that with the cords it was bound about the waist.
>
> This robe Nicodemus presented then to the Master, Jesus, after the healing of the widow of Nain's son, who was a relative of Nicodemus.
>
> In the activities, then, when Nicodemus went to the Master by night and there became those discussions in the home, for Nicodemus and Martha there began the communion as man and wife rather than man and his chattel or his servant. They were more on a basis of equality, not in the same proportions which were established a bit later by some of the rulers from the Roman land but more in keeping with the happenings which had brought about the activities in the Essenes group.
>
> Though Martha was an Essene, Nicodemus never accepted completely the tenets or the teachings of the Essenes group. These were a part of the principles and applications of Martha. 3175-3

In 1947, [3175] married a professional writer and began to travel throughout the county with him. According to notations on file, she remained an active member of the A.R.E. even into the 1960s.

Noah

(also known as Noe)
Genesis 5-10; I Chronicles 1:4; Isaiah 54:9; Ezekiel 14:12-23; Matthew 24:37-38; Luke 3:36, 17:26-27; Hebrews 11:7; I Peter 3:20; II Peter 2:5
Case 2547

Noah is best known for being the patriarch of the Deluge. According to the Bible, when the earth was vile and filled with corruption, Noah found grace in the eyes of God and was given instructions for building an ark to survive the Great Flood. When he was about five hundred years old, his three sons were born: Shem, Ham, and Japheth. One hundred years later he was given the ark instructions and told to gather a pair of every living species to take into the ark. (One account of the Genesis story holds that seven pairs of "clean" animals were gathered along with one pair of "unclean" animals.) When Noah and his wife, his sons, and his sons' wives had gathered into the ark, it rained for forty days and forty nights. Because the waters of the Flood had covered the earth, Noah and his family stayed aboard the craft for approximately one year. After disembarking and being told to replenish the earth, Noah discovered the fermentation process for grapes and apparently became the first individual to become drunk.

Between 1939 and 1944, a number of individuals received life readings and were told that they had been members of Noah's immediate family. (See also "Japheth," "Maran," "Methuselah," "Rezepatha," and "Shelobothe.") One of the most impressive was a reading for a young boy who had not yet reached the age of four. His parents were told that the child had been the Protestant reformer, Thomas Campbell, the prophet Elisha (see also "Elisha"), and the patriarch of the Deluge:

Here we may see a demonstration, an illustration of that which has been indicated or intimated through these channels, as of a *perfect* channel being formed for the advent of an entity-soul that would bring blessings to all—*if* there is the directing of the developing years.

The responsibility, then, rests with the mother, the father, for the next eight years. There will then be given, here, those studies. For, it will be easy to teach him Greek. It will be easy to teach him those things that were portions of the activity.

For, before *that* the entity was that one to whom was entrusted man's advent into the world—Noah.

From this we find those weaknesses. Then, not as one refraining from those, but beware ever of any strong drink or fruit of the vine passing the lips of *this* entity—through these early periods, especially.

Do these, and we will find blessings to man—through this entity . . .

Let this be the prayer with the entity, daily:

"Father, God! In Thy love, in Thy mercy, Thou hast given us the opportunity to see the manifestations of Thy love among men. Let us appreciate that opportunity Thou hast given. And may each of us, day by day, keep the faith in Him who has promised, 'Lo, I am with thee always, even unto the end of the world.'" 2547-1

Cayce told the parents that their son had abilities as a speaker and a minister. One of the first reports on file is from 1948 when an uncle stated that the boy seemed to have an awareness of the weather, warning his parents of approaching storms on several occasions long before anyone else saw any signs. Later, he and his wife became very active in their church. The last report is from 1963 when it was reported that [2547] had become a manager of a large chain supermarket in the small Southern town where he lived.

Reuben

Genesis 29:32, 30:14-20, 35:21-26, 37, 42, 46:8-9, 48:5, 49; Exodus 1:1-5, 6:14; Numbers 1, 2, 7:30-35, 10:18, 13:4, 16:1-5, 26:3-7; 32, 34:13-15; Deuteronomy 11:1-7, 27:11-15, 33:4-7; Joshua 4:12-13, 13, 15:6, 18, 20:8, 21:7, 21:36, 22; Judges 5:15; I Chronicles 2:1-2, 5:1-3, 5:18, 6:63-81; Ezekiel 48; Revelation 7
Case 693

Jacob was the father of twelve sons who would eventually become leaders of the twelve tribes of Israel. One of those sons was Reuben, the eldest son of Jacob and Leah; another was Joseph, Jacob's favorite. Reuben's birthright as firstborn was forfeited because of his affair with Bilhah, his father's concubine. Even though Reuben realized how his father felt about his younger brother, Joseph, when his other brothers became enraged with jealousy, he talked his brothers out of killing Joseph. He also tried to save the young man from being sold into slavery and became deeply saddened when it appeared that Joseph had disappeared for good. During the famine in Canaan, he moved with the rest of his family to Egypt. Years later, he would wander the desert with Moses in search of the Promised Land. (See also "Benjamin.")

The mother of an eleven-year-old boy, who had received several readings for epilepsy, obtained a life reading for him in 1935. Though he was partially paralyzed and unable to care for himself properly, the mother was told that her son had the opportunity to have much of his illness eradicated as long as they worked together for healing before he became fourteen. If her son had not been healed by that time, the condition would remain throughout his adult life.

Apparently, in the boy's most recent incarnation in Salem, he had used others for his own physical gratification, taking sexual advantage of individuals who were incarcerated, suppressed, or belittled by society. During the time of Jesus, he had both lost and gained spiritually as a member of the Sanhedrin who represented the tribe of Reuben. Prior to that lifetime, he had been Reuben himself:

> Before that we find the entity was among the first born of Jacob and Leah, and making for the expressions that in the beginning brought much that was in accord with the callings into an activity where these might have brought the blessings upon the activities in the sojourn. Yet when the desires of the flesh entered, and the associations with those things and about those peoples that had been as an expression of intolerance to those peoples, the entity made for the associations that brought disorder, discontent within those of its own household and those of its people in that experience and that expression.
>
> These made for again those activities that have brought in the present the necessity of the awareness of the spiritual awakening within the expression and experience of the entity. 693-3

He also had an earlier incarnation in the Tigris-Euphrates area at the time when individuals were first accepting the idea of polygamy. Apparently, that tendency had remained with him at a soul level. The mother was reminded that there was a purposeful experience that she and her son were being drawn together. The foremost lesson she was encouraged to teach him was simply as follows: "As ye would that men should do to you, do ye even so to them." Provided the boy learned that lesson, he would experience great growth in this particular incarnation and he would have a very constructive lifetime. Finally, she was encouraged to help her son find harmony—physically, mentally, and spiritually.

After following the suggestions outlined in [693]'s physical readings, the mother and chiropractor both noticed improvements in the child's physical condition. His convulsions had greatly decreased and his speech was improving. After a period of great improvement, however, [693] seemed to have a setback a few months later and his convulsions returned. No additional follow-up reports are on file.

Rezepatha
Genesis 6-10
Case 2425

According to the Book of Genesis, Noah, his wife, his sons, and his sons' wives all entered into an ark of their own construction in order to survive the Great Flood. Although not mentioned specifically by name in the Bible, between 1939 and 1944 various individuals received life readings and were told that they had been members of Noah's immediate family. Those people included Noah's three daughters-in-law who, Cayce stated, were named Maran, Rezepatha, and Shelobothe. (See also "Japheth," "Maran," "Methuselah," "Noah," and "Shelobothe.") Cayce stated that Noah's family was *one* of those who had survived the Deluge; there had been others as well. According to the Bible, after the Flood all of Noah's sons' wives had children and helped replenish the earth.

A twenty-one-year-old housewife who had been practicing automatic writing learned that she and her husband had also been married during the time of Noah.

During that period, she had been named Rezepatha, her husband had been Japheth, and she had accompanied him on the ark:

> Before that the entity was in that activity when there were those preparations for changes being wrought in the relationships of Creative Forces with the sons of men.
>
> The entity was among those, or that one chosen by Japheth as the companion in the ark.
>
> With the relationships to that activity, the entity finds within self the visions of changes, in the relationships that are again soon to be established by and through the elements themselves in their dealing with man and Creative Forces or God's laws.
>
> The name then was Rezepatha. 2425-1

Mrs. [2425] was told that she had also lived in Delaware just prior to the American Revolution and had been among those who had championed freedom. According to the reading, at the time she had been both a homebuilder and a builder of the nation. She learned that she had also been among the Essenes and one of the daughters trained and raised as a potential channel for the Messiah. At that time, she had been very psychic and able to attune to higher forces. Later, she had been present at the Crucifixion. In ancient Persia, she had been a seeker who became acquainted with the "city in the hills and the plains." Unfortunately, she had lost when she turned what she had learned in that lifetime into selfish personal gain.

Her reading stated that one of her abilities was that she could assist others in becoming aware of their relationship to the Divine. Told not to be merely interested in psychic phenomena, she was encouraged to seek true religious experiences like those that had been a part of her life in the past. Her soul strengths included purity, a strong intellect, and personal sincerity. She possessed abilities as a homemaker, a teacher, a writer, or an artist. Cayce advised her that her life would provide her with experiences enabling her to learn the beautiful influence of love in an individual's life.

After receiving the reading, Mrs. [2425] wrote Mr. Cayce: "Through this guidance I shall truly enter my inner temple and receive therein the guidance of divine law, that I may fulfill my purposes in this life. I send you my blessing for giving me what is beyond measure the greatest inspiration I have ever had." That same year, her mother-in-law reported that she was extremely grateful for her daughter-in-law and believed [2425] had come into their family to save it and hold it together. Over the next two years, she gave birth to two sons, one of whom was told that he had been born to her as her son on the ark. Her baby's nurse would also receive a reading and discover that she had been Rezepatha's mother during the Noah incarnation.

She and her husband separated in 1946. Later [2425] married and had two more sons. In 1954, she told Gladys Davis that she had a recent psychic experience in which Edgar Cayce had appeared to help her in a time of need. A letter in 1956 stated that her second husband had left her: "My second marriage ended much as my first. This is far sadder than death to see a loved one lose himself, but perhaps through this he will come up, and only this experience with us could make the impression—he learned to believe in others, now he must learn to believe in himself . . . "

In 1960 she reported that she was teaching first grade. In 1970 her first mother-in-law stated that [2425] "has had such a terrible life." However, in 1999, friends of [2425] reported that she was still very active and had remained an enthusiast, a supporter, and a volunteer for the Cayce work all her life. She frequently travels and still enjoys entertaining guests in her New England home.

Ruth
Book of Ruth; Matthew 1:5
Case 5256

Ruth was the faithful daughter-in-law who chose to accompany her mother-in-law, Naomi, to Bethlehem after both were widowed and on the verge of starvation. (See also "Naomi.") While in Bethlehem, Ruth scoured the fields in search of food and attracted the attention of Boaz, a wealthy landowner. (See also "Boaz.") They eventually married and had a son, Obed, who would become David's grandfather.

Edgar Cayce began the life reading for a seventeen-year-old girl by stating that the "possibilities and probabilities are very beautiful for this entity." She was encouraged to live in such a manner that others would wish to be more like her. Because she had a good singing and speaking voice, she was advised to pursue music not as a career but personally. Wondering about her marital future, she was told that as she pursued music, she would draw to herself the appropriate associations and relationships. Worried about her weight, she was encouraged to pursue outdoor activities such as golf, riding, swimming, and tennis. These activities would also assist her in becoming more outgoing socially.

Her most recent incarnation was as an Indian maiden in the Connecticut area, where she had acquired a great instinct for the outdoors. At the same time she developed a feeling of inferiority and an innate loneliness which had led to a deep desire for companionship. Prior to the Indian incarnation, she had been Ruth:

> Before that we find the entity was in the Holy

Land and the entity was among those who went, who gave self as a sacrifice for a cause and a purpose. There the entity found strength, just as in the experience in the present.

While persecutions brought to the entity, then as Ruth, a fear of loneliness, and if it could just be alone in the present, and from those experiences, this combination. What the entity promises it keeps, and it is naturally hard for the entity to tell a lie. Don't practice it! For "what a fatal web ye weave when first ye practice to deceive."

In that experience then the entity gained, though not in long periods of years. Yet in the individuality, while manifested in the entity's personality then, shines a reserve.

Know in whom ye have believed, as ye did as Ruth, and know that He is able to keep that ye have committed unto Him against any experience which may arise in thy life. 5256-1

In ancient Egypt she had been among those first trained in the establishment of individual homes for the rearing of children, rather than the previous system in which the state took over that function.

In the present, [5256] was encouraged to have as part of her life music, literature, design, and the great outdoors. She was told that she could make a career in interior decoration and that by her twenty-first birthday she would have begun her family. She was advised not to become discouraged, to trust in God, and to take the time to be holy, gracious, and patient, "even with those who apparently would hurt you." As she did these, she would make a great contribution to the world. Shortly thereafter, her mother noted that they were grateful for the life reading as well as for a physical reading for the child's father.

No response was received to a follow-up questionnaire that was mailed in 1949.

Ruth, Jesus' Sister
Matthew 13:53-58; Mark 6:1-5
Case 1158

Although she was not specifically mentioned in the Bible, Edgar Cayce stated that Jesus had a younger sister named Ruth, who had been born after Mary and Joseph had begun normal marital relations. In fact, Cayce contended that a number of years after Jesus had been born of a virgin, the couple had several children, including sons named James and Jude. (See also "Jude.") The readings state that Ruth was raised among the Essene community and often heard about the expectations for her older brother, Jesus, who had left the family to be educated in such places as Egypt and the Far East. When He returned for His ministry, Ruth was numbered among His followers. She would eventually marry a Roman citizen, with whom she would have a family, and spend much of her time in Rome.

A forty-six-year-old housewife obtained her first life reading in 1936 and was told that one of her past-life experiences was so outstanding that it overshadowed the rest of them. That experience had been as Ruth, the sister of Jesus. Additional incarnations had included being the daughter of a physician during the American Revolution. At that time she aided those who fought in the war. When independence had been won, for the rest of her life she lived as an example of harmony and hope to those around her. Previously, she had been among the Greeks who had ventured into the "city in the hills and plains" in Persia.

A short time after the reading, Mrs. [1158] requested follow-up information on her lifetime as Ruth. She learned that Jesus had studied in Egypt and in Persia during the time of her youth and returned years later when Joseph died. She and her brother, Jesus, met for the first time at Joseph's funeral. Although she felt much love for her elder brother, according to the readings it was hard for [1158] to understand everything people said about Him, including the virgin birth.

> Hence the entity, Ruth, was rather in awe of the suggestions, the intimations that surrounded that experience; and questioned the mother concerning same.
>
> As the entity grew into maidenhood, and after the birth of Jude, then the death of Joseph brought that brother—Jesus—home! and there were those activities that surrounded the entity concerning that unknown, that strange kinsman; that kinsman whom the peoples held in awe, yet said many unkind things about Him.
>
> With the departure of that brother to Egypt for the final initiations or teachings, with John [the Baptist]—another kinsman who had been spoken of and held in awe, his mother having been a chosen vessel by the priests of the Essenes, and he, John, being the lineal descendent of the high priests of the Jews—we find that in the entity's latter teen ages such ponderings brought a great many disturbing influences to the entity, Ruth . . .
>
> Then the return of Jesus to the Palestine land, after those periods of the tests in the wilderness, after His meeting with John; and then the return to Capernaum and the teachings that He, Jesus, accorded there.
>
> The entity then for the first time heard in the synagogue His first utterances, as to the prophesies of Isaiah, Jeremiah, and the teachings of the lesser

prophets, and as to how they applied in the experiences of that day. 1158-4

Mrs. [1158] was told that she had been married to her present husband in that incarnation and that Jesus had attended her wedding. It was while she was in Rome that the Crucifixion occurred, and she returned to join with her mother and the other holy women.

Cayce told [1158] that she still possessed the innate awareness of His teachings and an understanding of His work that could be awakened within herself through introspection. She was encouraged to keep foremost in her mind, "As ye do it unto the least of thy brethren, ye do it unto thy Maker."

Until Edgar Cayce's death in 1945, Mrs. [1158] was a strong supporter of the readings and obtained thirty-eight for herself. Her husband and children received readings as well, so there are literally hundreds of pages of follow-up reports and correspondence on file, much of it expressing appreciation for Cayce's work.

Even after Cayce's death, Mrs. [1158] and her husband were very involved in the Association. In 1949, her husband died just seven months after celebrating their twenty-fifth wedding anniversary.

A report from 1963 states that she was in good health and enjoying her grandchildren. For the next twenty years, Mrs. [1158] stayed connected with the A.R.E. and took part in occasional lectures and consented to be interviewed about her readings for books and articles. A notation from 1989 states: "Although she has cataracts and is no longer able to drive, Mrs. [1158] remains socially as well as politically active . . . She will celebrate her one-hundredth birthday in February 1990." She visited A.R.E. the following year. Amazingly, she lived until February 1999, just shy of her one-hundred-and-ninth birthday.

Saul

I Samuel 9-11, 13-29, 31; II Samuel 1-7, 9, 12, 16, 19, 21-22; I Chronicles 5:10, 8:28-40, 9:35-44, 10-12, 13:1-4, 15:28-29, 26:27-28; Isaiah 10:27-29

Case 221

The first king of Israel, Saul was summoned to lead the people against the Philistines by the prophet Samuel. An energetic and courageous man, Saul also possessed an imposing physical presence. For a time, he was known as the "goodliest person" in all of Israel. After his initial successes as ruler, however, he became prone to periods of depression, irrationality, and extreme jealousy. A young musician named David could calm Saul's nerves, but when David became more popular with the people, Saul grew even more irrational and attempted to have David killed. Because Saul no longer followed the will of God, Samuel anointed David as the next king of Israel—a prophecy that would come to pass years later after Samuel had died. Saul was eventually killed in a battle with the Philistines, as predicted by Samuel's ghost when Saul visited the witch of Endor for an audience with the deceased prophet.

The Edgar Cayce readings spoke of the great potential possessed by the soul who had been Saul. In fact, Cayce believed that Saul could have become the greatest leader of the Jewish people. Unfortunately, due to the misuse of his free will and the erroneous choices he made, Saul was not able to measure up to his spiritual potential. In spite of high ideals, the soul was weak in applying them. Interestingly enough, although it was not mentioned in the life reading for the individual told he had been Saul, a side comment in a reading given in 1940 to the Glad Helpers Prayer Group (281-48) indicated that Saul had also incarnated as Benjamin, the second son of Jacob and Rachel. (See also "Benjamin.") Another reading (5148-2) stated that Saul had also been Seth, the third son of Adam and Eve. (See also "Seth.")

A thirty-year-old oil prospector received one of the earliest life readings in 1924 and was advised that he would do well to keep his life focused on the straight and narrow path. He was also told that he had been in Greece during a period when the materialists had taken control of the government and he had been among the governing minority. Earlier, he had been Saul:

> In that before we find the entity as that of the leader as chosen for the first king [Saul] in and with the chosen people, and was the herder as sought the lost animals of his father when appointed as the leader. [1 Sam. 9:2; 11:15] Hence we find in this present sphere those elements bringing through in this personality and individuality those as in this:
>
> In the first the one chosen of the higher elements. Hence ever those forces about this entity where, though all others fail, this one may, through direct self-control, gain those forces of the higher and highest realms in the present plane.
>
> In the second that force as is manifested in the great thoughts and ideals builded about self, yet ever just beyond carrying those to execution. May be done by sheer will and by adhering to those immutable laws that give self the insight of the forces that lend to the upbuilding of all force relative to the higher elements. 221-2

His reading also stated that he was often intellectual in his approach to things. Immediately after giving the information, Edgar Cayce wrote: "When you have studied this over quite seriously and earnestly, I'd like for you to give me your honest and candid opinion relative to its contents and its applicability to you." Mr. [221] never responded to the letter.

Seth
Genesis 4:25-26, 5:1-8; I Chronicles 1:1; Luke 3:38
Case 221

Seth was the third son of Adam and Eve, born after the murder of his brother Abel. All that is known of him is that he was a forefather of the Israel nation, a father of Enosh, and that he lived to be 912 years old.

In 1944, during the course of a life reading given to a fifty-five-year-old writer and housewife (5148-2), Cayce stated that Saul had been a gifted and "goodly king," but he had allowed himself to forget his humbleness because of his exalted position. His humility, however, had enabled that same soul to be the channel of the chosen people and the forefather to Abraham, Isaac, and Jacob, for Saul had once been Seth. (See also "Saul.") Mr. [221]'s own life reading did not mention his Seth incarnation, but it did mention his incarnation as Benjamin. (See also "Benjamin.")

Shelobothe
Genesis 6-10
Case 2624

According to the Book of Genesis, Noah, his wife, his sons, and his sons' wives all entered into an ark of their own construction in order to survive the Great Flood. Although not mentioned specifically by name in the Bible, between 1939 and 1944 various individuals received life readings and were told that they had been members of Noah's immediate family. Those people included Noah's three daughters-in-law who, Cayce stated, were named Maran, Rezepatha, and Shelobothe. (See also "Japheth,"

"Maran," "Methuselah," "Noah," and "Rezepatha.") Cayce contended that Noah's family was *one* of those who had survived the Deluge; there had been others as well. According to the Bible, after the Flood all of Noah's sons' wives had children and helped replenish the earth.

A forty-one-year-old woman cook, who had been born in Scotland, was reminded that each incarnation in the earth had the opportunity to be a purposeful experience. Told that her lifetimes had been quite varied, in her most recent experience she had lived in Virginia during the creation of the colonies and had been a seamstress preparing a variety of cloth and material needed for the home. From that experience, she gained an ability to be helpful in any endeavor that assisted individuals in preparing or establishing their own homes.

Before that, she had lived in Scotland during a period of conflict between the Scots, the Welsh, and the English. Although she had attempted to bring calmness out of chaos, she was banished to France for her activities. From that incarnation she possessed an innate desire for freedom. In the Holy Land, she was a close friend of Martha of Bethany and had come to know Jesus because of His visits to the home of Martha, Mary, and Lazarus. She had also been present for the burial and resurrection of Lazarus, after which she became one of the Holy Women and a follower of Jesus. In ancient Egypt she had been born to Atlantean parents and helped individuals discover their true vocation. She had also lived during the time of the Great Flood:

> Before that, in those periods when there were the activities in the land such that there had come those determinations for the bringing about of the destruction of the wickedness of the world—the entity was among those that were saved.
>
> For the entity then was the companion of Shem,

> that first brought the activities to Noah in that experience.
>
> Thus in the present experience, though separated in activities from those of its own people, the entity has brought life, health and peace to others. So may the entity in the present, through its present activities, bring those influences that will make for the regeneration of those things and turmoils that are in the earth today.
>
> The name then was Shelobothe. 2624-1

In the present, [2624] was encouraged to cultivate the same faith she had found in Bethany. According to her reading, she could serve best working with groups of individuals, assisting and directing them to know "the ways of life." When she asked why she felt so emotionally distant from members of her own family, she was told that it was because some of them had been the ones responsible for her banishment.

Immediately after receiving the reading, [2624] remarked that she was truly overcome because it explained so much about herself that she had never been able to understand. No additional follow-up reports are on file.

Sheluenmehei
II Samuel 5:13, 12:1-25
Case 601

King David was the second and most famous king of Israel, and made Jerusalem the political and religious capital of his kingdom. He had an adulterous affair with Bathsheba, the result of which was a child who died at birth. David and Bathsheba turned again to one another for comfort, and a second child was born. Although the Bible says that child was Solomon, Cayce stated that a girl had been born next and that her name was Sheluen-mehei, the daughter of David and Bathsheba. Her younger brother would become King Solomon.

A forty-eight-year-old Jewish housewife obtained her first life reading in 1934. It stated that she was extremely intuitive and would seldom be in error about her judgment of an individual's strengths and weaknesses. For that reason, she would be excellent working in personnel for a large organization or in choosing teachers or ministers for specific assignments. Although she was rather temperamental and could become easily angry, she also possessed talents as a diplomat and could bring harmony among individuals.

Her most recent incarnation had been in France, where she had chosen to immigrate to the United States after the French Revolution. In that lifetime she gained in her efforts to aid individuals in preparing soil and crops, but lost in terms of often suppressing others' personalities and thoughts in preference to her own. Prior to that she had been the widow of Nain, a woman at the time of Jesus, whose son had been raised from the dead by Jesus Himself. (See also "Widow of Nain.") Mrs. [601] learned that she had also been a daughter to King David:

> Before that we find (wherein much is made manifest in the present sojourn, present activities) the entity was during the reign of that ruler, that king of the Hebrew people who had been called for a purpose in a promised land; and among the daughters of David was the entity numbered; and among the daughters—or *the* daughter of Bathsheba that lived; hence a close relationship, and only mentioned once in the Scriptures—and only in a portion of so much that has been left out.
>
> So, the entity was a sister of Solomon—that also rose to the beauty of the pomp and power. This

> brought into the experience of the entity all those glories of the two kingdoms; for the entity was among those that were favored, not only of the people but of those that came for counsel—as the people of many nations—to receive, in those associations and relations, words of counsel from the preacher or the teacher in Solomon, and those *greater* in the Psalms of David.
>
> Hence many of these have been to the entity the songs wherein there has come within self much that has lifted up, especially in those instances when it is said, "I was glad when they said unto me, we will go into the house of our God." In this Psalm the entity led often in the meetings of those that counseled for the aid of those that would purify themselves for the services in the various activities. However, as is known, the mothers and daughters were forbidden much of the activities then.
>
> In the name then Sheluenmehei, the entity gained much in the experience, and aided the father during those days when Absalom the beautiful rebelled; during those days when darkness came to the peoples through the various changes wrought by the political forces and powers. 601-2

From that same experience as David's daughter, [601] became adept at judging political influences.

Finally, [601] was told that in ancient Egypt she had been extremely psychic and had worked in one of the temples, skilled in utilizing music for personal cleansing and attunement.

Cayce stated that even now she carried herself gracefully, as "a daughter of the king among kings." Although never imposing her views upon others, she was gracious in offering assistance in all her associations and relationships. In the present she could excel in any field that enabled others to experience soul development, physically, mentally, or spiritually. She possessed great talents in ministering to others and in enabling individuals to create a home environment.

After receiving the reading she wrote: "My reading amazed me. I have read it many times and will have to continue reading it many times more before I can thoroughly understand it. Many passages are accurate but much needs clarification. The general content makes me feel very humble and thankful that I can be of service to others." Over the next few years, she obtained additional readings for herself and other family members. A file notation states that her daughter's son was born dead in 1937, causing her much grief. Shortly thereafter Mrs. [601] developed uterine cancer and died on April 20, 1938.

A few weeks after [601] died, her daughter wrote: "The companionship and understanding she gave us—only she could give . . . the place she filled in our hearts and minds (mine and Daddy's) no one will ever know. We all seemed to live for one another."

Silas

(also known as Silvanus)
Acts 15:22-41, 16:11-40, 17, 18:1-6; II Corinthians 1:19; I Thessalonians 1:1; II Thessalonians 1:1; I Peter 5:12
Case 707

Originally part of the Christian sect at Jerusalem, Silas accompanied Paul on his second missionary journey. Like Paul, he was a Roman citizen. His travels took him through Asia Minor, Macedonia, Antioch, Beroea, Corinth, and Thessalonica. Eventually he assisted Peter in his work and carried one of Peter's letters to the churches in Asia Minor.

In 1934, a fifty-seven-year-old man received his first

reading and was advised that personal doubts and the desire to wander often affected him. Told that he possessed intuitive abilities, he was encouraged to facilitate his own soul's awakening in the manifestation of spiritual principles in the earth.

In his most recent life he had been an Indian medicine man near Talladega, Alabama, and had buried a treasure of jewels that still remained hidden. Prior to that, he had been married to a daughter of Martha and Nicodemus and was one of Jesus' closest followers:

> Before that we find the entity was in that land now known as the Roman and the Grecian, in those periods when there were the gatherings of those that partook of those understandings, tenets and teachings of the man of Galilee.
>
> The entity was among those that were His close followers, among those that knew the powers and the might of those influences in the experience; for the entity—with Paul, with Barnabas—learned of those manifestations that had come to the sons of men; suffering in body—as Silas, that ye have read of, that ye have loved as ye read, that ye have understood better than ye have many of those. For thou wert the companion of Luke, and Mark—who was the recorder of the first of those things that were dictated by his own uncle, Peter, who gave to thee strength. Though in bonds, thou hast seen them fall away. Though in poverty, thou hast seen all the good things of the earth, all good things of the spirit, poured out upon the sons of men! Hold thou, mine brother, mine friend, to those things that thou gavest to thy fellow man in that day! Let him that was thy guide, let him that was thy teacher, *still* come to thee. Open again the doors that thou may see the glories of the Lord as thou usest thy voice, as

> thou raisest that night in the prison when the doors were opened, as thou sawest the Romans made afraid. Then may thou feel within thine inner self those bonds of doubt and fear, that have at times taken possession of thee, fade even as the darkness from those prison walls faded—as there was the light of the countenance of the Son of man that makes men free indeed shed abroad in thine self in that body thou wore during that experience. *Such glory* that the bars were severed, the doors were opened, and all spoke the *glory* of God! Thou may make manifest such in this material world, wilt thou *hold fast* to that thou hast gained in that experience as Silas, the helpmeet of him to whom was given the keys of the kingdom in the earth, who made that declaration of all declarations to his brethren as they walked, "Thou art Him who has been sent from God that we might know that His love may sustain men in their trials, in their tribulations, in their joys, in their sorrows, in their weakness; yea, even in their might. Thou, O God, *art* the Giver of life, and light, and understanding!" *Hold* to that, my friend, my brother. 707-1

Previous to his life as Silas, he had been father to the leader and healer who helped found "the city in the hills and the plains." According to the reading, in that incarnation [707] possessed healing ability and assisted others though prayer and the laying on of hands. He was encouraged to tap this ability in the present, remembering that he was simply being used as a channel through which the Creative Forces could manifest. In ancient Egypt he had been one of the priests working in the Temple of Sacrifice, a native who had originally rebelled against the high priest but would eventually become one of his biggest supporters.

In the present, he was encouraged to awaken to the same faith that had been his during his incarnation as Silas. After the reading, it was noted that Mr. [707] said that he had found what he had always been seeking: a sense of freedom in doing God's will. Later, he became more involved in healing and the laying on of hands. Regarding his abilities, a report from 1936 noted: "A few weeks ago a man was arrested here because his car was throwing off a volume of smoke, and was to appear at court the next morning. That night Mr. [707] prayed for the man, and when the man went to court the next morning the judge said the case had been thrown out of court."

After his reading, Mr. [707] became increasingly interested in discovering the treasure he had once buried in Alabama. He obtained two readings specifically on finding it. He was told that, although the proximity of the location could be given, he could only find the treasure if he rededicated himself in service to God and managed to live in the same manner he had done when he once walked with Jesus. A file notation from 1937 states that Mr. [707] and his wife later spent quite a bit of time searching for the treasure but to no avail; they became rather downhearted about the whole situation. He and his wife also obtained a joint reading on their past-life relationship.

The last notation is from 1970. The woman who had been Nicodemus's wife in the past reported an experience she had after looking at a photograph in Mr. Cayce's office:

> . . . I spoke to Gladys about one of the photographs high on the wall of Mr. Cayce's reading room. The photo was the one photo which held my interest. I thought it was because the man of the photo resembled someone I knew and I could not bring to

mind who he was. Gladys told me the man's name and the state of his residence, but that didn't help me any. Then, as she started to leave the room she turned and exclaimed, " . . . that man was told he was Silas, so he would have been your son-in-law in your Palestine incarnation." Since then I have thought many times of how almost unbelievable it was that I . . . would have a remembrance of a man I knew in another lifetime, from a *photograph* of that man as he is in this incarnation.

Silvanus
Luke 10
Case 1529

Although not mentioned specifically by name in the Bible, Silvanus, according to Cayce, was one of the seventy disciples appointed by Jesus to spread His work by ministering, counseling, and healing. The readings stated that Silvanus often assisted the apostles and gave counsel to the Church's early bishops and deacons.

A sixty-two-year-old doctor of philosophy, teacher, and minister sought assistance from Edgar Cayce. Referred by a friend, he was frequently overwhelmed by the numbers of people in his congregation who had difficulties and clung to him, sapping his own vitality. When the problem became severe, he frequently developed asthma as a result. He decided to obtain a life reading.

The reading was given in 1938 and acknowledged that Doctor [1529] had not had an easy time. However, much of his work had enabled him to experience an "at-onement" with spiritual forces. Told that he was an effective counselor, he was advised by Cayce that, whenever he felt overcome by his work, to simply separate himself from others—just as Jesus had done—in order to make time to purify and regenerate himself.

His reading stated that only a few of his incarnations were having a major influence on his present life. In a prior incarnation he had defended the Holy Land as an English warrior in the Crusades. Although he had been strong in faith, he had acquired many doubts as to whether or not his physical needs would be met in that experience. Those same doubts and fears arose in the present when he became overwhelmed by his work. Before that experience, he had been one of the seventy disciples appointed to carry out Jesus' ministry:

> Before that we find the entity lived during that period when the Master walked in the earth, and when there were those gatherings about the Disciples and the followers, and when the Master blessed the Seventy that were to go abroad and teach and minister to others and preach repentance, that the day of the Lord was at hand.
>
> Ye then were among that Seventy, and again on the days or Day of Pentecost ye rededicated thyself—as Silvanus.
>
> And as a teacher and a minister in the churches of lower Asia and the upper portions of the Palestine land, ye ministered to thy fellow men; and gained and *gained* through those experiences; bringing encouragement and hope and faith again and again into the hearts and minds and experiences of those that from the very stumbling forces of life from the political and social and economic forces became weak and stumbling.
>
> And indeed to thee may it be accredited that in Caesarea were those followers first called Christ-like, or Christ-ians!
>
> In thy associations with the Twelve, the bishops, the deacons, ye brought counsel and strength. 1529-1

He also had an earlier incarnation during the period of Ezra, when the Jews had returned to Jerusalem to build the city. At that time, he had been an aid to Ezra, interpreting the law. From that experience he realized how spiritual tenets were to be lived and not merely known. In ancient Egypt, he assisted individuals in their worship, but had often been discouraged by the people's lack of personal application. In that same lifetime, he had also worked as a tiller of the soil and a harvester of crops.

Dr. [1529] was advised that his work in the present was to assist those who came to him for aid. Within himself he possessed the "desire to bring into the hearts of men again and again *hope,* encouragement; and to *sow* again and again the seed that [would] bear the fruits of the Spirit—patience, gentleness, kindness, brotherly love, long-suffering!" He was encouraged to help and to inspire people in their own personal development. Relief from his asthma could be obtained through physical adjustments and by becoming less personally affected by others' problems.

Five years later, Dr. [1529] wrote Hugh Lynn Cayce after the publication of *There Is a River.* He stated that he had never paid that much attention to his reading and really did not know what he had until that book and *A Search for God, Book I,* were published. In 1950, after reading *Many Mansions* by Gina Cerminara he wrote: "*Many Mansions* has opened the doors of my thought to the reasonableness of both of these principles [karma and reincarnation] and has through the evidence drawn from the Cayce manuscripts forced me to see that these principles are not only reasonable, but that the evidence here presented shows them to be inevitably present in the wider universe around us."

In 1951 he requested a copy of his reading: "I have lost the original copy and would be most happy to review it and to find what new lessons may come out of it now that the years have rolled around. I know that it did help me tremendously at the moment and led to my being entirely free from the difficulties about which I had written."

The final notation is from 1952 when Gladys Davis wrote that Dr. [1529] and his wife had been very helpful with A.R.E. programs that had come to their area.

Thaddeus

(also known as Judas and Lebbaeus; also spelled Thaddaeus)
Matthew 10:1-4; Mark 3:14-19; Luke 6:13-16; John 14:22-24; Acts 1:12-14
Case 361

Thaddeus is considered one of the least known of the twelve apostles. The son of James, he was also called Judas (not Iscariot). Beyond the listing of his name, the only statement attributed to him from Scripture occurs at the Last Supper when he asks how Jesus would reveal Himself to them.

A young man who had previously obtained some physical readings for problems with malnutrition received a life reading in 1934 at the age of fifteen. His reading stated that he had a great mind and could be called a visionary because of his ability see things hidden from others. However, he also had a tendency toward procrastination, putting off what he knew needed to be accomplished. Cayce reminded him, "Dreams are wonderful, yet these only dreamed do not come to pass." Easily prone to anger, he was counseled to learn to govern his temper rather than suppressing it. He was also interested in metaphysics and had had quite a number of psychic experiences.

The young man was told that his most recent incarnation had been among the English settlers who had journeyed to Jamestown in 1607. Originally planning to be a minister, he became one of those in authority after the establishment of the colonies. From that incarnation he also possessed the innate desire to make the sea and exploration a part of his life. His reading stated that he had also been alive when the Prince of Peace was in the earth:

> The entity followed with the Master in those activities, in the name then Thaddeus, among those that were chosen as a light bearer to a people that had been shown a light as shining into the darkness of those periods.
>
> Through that experience the entity gained, though oft was among those that were weighing well the material gains to be had; yet gaining throughout the sojourn, for it was among those who came under the sound of the Voice and heard, "Believe ye not for my words, for the very works' sake believe ye!"
>
> Then, from that experience in the present, those things whether of the mystic forces, the material world or of the spiritual import that come to the entity should ever be weighed well with—and bear the mark of—the judgment set by Him: "As ye do it unto the least of these, my brethren, ye do it unto me." These *are* innately, manifestedly, the judgments of the body. Hold fast to that thou hast gained in this judgment—of the world, for the judge of this world cometh and there will be light again found in Him, and thou may be in that position as thou wert in that land—as a light, as a guide, to him that may be the messenger of the King coming to His own! 361-4

Additional past lives had been in Persia, where he had rebelled against those in power but had eventually served as a messenger of truth to his people. In ancient Egypt, he was a member of the priesthood and assisted individuals in their purification of body and mind. In the present, he was encouraged to manifest his abilities in such a way that they glorified his relationship to the Creative Forces. His best line of work would be in any field that dealt with the relationships of individuals to one another.

After receiving the reading, [361] stated that he was proud of it and felt that it was going to mean a great deal to him. Cayce gave him another reading as a high school graduation present in 1937, which commented on his choice of colleges, his educational plans, and encouraged him to pursue working in public service. In 1940, [361] submitted a follow-up letter:

> My life reading described my characteristics, temperaments, and emotions perfectly. In fact, I began to feel that I was beginning to get acquainted with myself. In fact, I might say that every time I now read it over, I can check another statement and recognize at once that it is I the reading is talking about. As to the help, I am unable to make a perfect statement. So far it has helped me more than anything I have ever read. It has made the Bible more understandable, but the true value of my life reading lies ahead of me. I, only, am responsible whether it is my priceless guide or proves worthless to me.

Additional file notations state that he joined the army during World War II and rose in rank to a master sergeant. He also married. In 1954 his mother said that he had become a house painter and was still very interested in the work of A.R.E. He and his wife had three sons; they were all very active in Sunday school. His hobby was farming and home gardening. One of the final notations about him is from 1967 when a family friend noted that Mr. [361] had in recent years begun selling life insurance and was doing very well.

Thesea
Matthew 2; Luke 1:5
Case 2067

Herod the Great was appointed by the Romans to rule Judea after his father's assassination. Unscrupulous and dictatorial, he was the supreme ruler and executed members of his own family, including a wife, Mariamne, and a favorite son in order to guarantee his position. He also ordered the death of the Innocents, killing all male babies in Bethlehem under the age of two to insure that the predicted Jewish Messiah would not interfere with his rule. Throughout his life, he would go through a series of wives, one of whom—according to Edgar Cayce—was a woman named Thesea to whom he was married at the time of the visit of the Wise Men.

A fifty-two-year-old doctor of philosophy and minister had attended a number of lectures given by Hugh Lynn and Edgar Cayce in New York. The head of the sociology department at her college, she obtained a life reading in 1939 and a follow-up reading in 1940. She was told that both her desire and her innate skill were to be used as a channel through which hope, help, and aid could come to others. Her reading stated that she appreciated beauty in all of its manifestations and could excel as a writer or as an observer of men and women in their various cultures and activities.

In her most recent incarnation, she had been in Salem, Massachusetts, and had been persecuted as a witch because of the visions she had and the psychic experiences she encountered. She lost her life at an early age because she had been dipped so frequently that she caught pneumonia and died of a fever. The reading stated that her ex-husband in the present had been one of those had who dipped her. She had also lived in Palestine at the time of Jesus:

> During those periods the entity was a queen of no mean estate, and took hold upon the words of the Master—though never personally coming in contact with Him. For the entity then was the companion or wife of Herod, who sought His destruction. Yet the entity's experience there, as Thesea, sought a closer comprehending of the Wise Men . . .
>
> For as the entity reasoned with the Essenes, as well as conversed with the Wise Men who came with the new messages to the world, the entity proclaimed—yea, that pronouncement that He Himself then being announced had given—"Others may do as they may, but as for me and my house, we will serve the living God." 2067-1

Chosen to be Herod's wife for political reasons when she was only fourteen years old, through her early training she was acquainted with many in the Essene community. That training gave her knowledge of numerous religious movements so that during her life as Thesea she wrote a historical summary of the experiences that occurred during the sojourn of the Jewish people. Cayce told her that this account had once been stored in the library at Alexandria and was destroyed along with the library. In Egypt, she had been one of Pharaoh's daughters during the time of Joseph and had been involved in founding what might be called "the Society of Magicians." In Indo-China she was a priestess who gave her people an understanding of the one God. In an earlier incarnation in ancient Egypt, [2067] was instrumental in establishing hospitals and schools.

In the present, she was encouraged to teach others by precept and example and advised that she could serve best by ministering, writing, and lecturing. In 1940, she wrote Edgar Cayce:

> I just can't refrain from writing you a little note at this time to tell you how much I have been helped during my visit at Virginia Beach. It has been the greatest privilege of my life to sit at your feet and to learn of the immensities of our God. You and yours have helped me solve the many great puzzles of my life. Before my visit I simply could not see the connection between many very important facts in the universe. You have not only enlarged my vision but synthesized it, with the result that my whole outlook on life and religion has changed. I have to thank you for this great enlightenment. I am convinced that your work is of universal import and under divine guidance.

Later notations from those who knew her stated that Dr. [2067] often suffered a "martyr complex," going from job to job in educational institutions because of it. Over the next few years, she would receive a dozen readings about her health, about books she wished to write, and about her plans for a ministry. She also referred a number of individuals for readings of their own. Since she was an enthusiastic writer, much of her correspondence is on file; however, no long-term follow-up reports were ever submitted.

Titus

II Corinthians 2:12-13, 7:5-16, 8, 12:18; Galatians 2; II Timothy 4:9; Titus 1:1-4

Case 1842

The recipient of one of St. Paul's epistles, Titus was a Greek converted to Christianity by Paul and would become one of his most trusted and able assistants. Paul refused to allow Titus to be circumcised in order to demonstrate that it was faith that saved an individual, not any ritualistic practice. Titus was especially helpful in straightening out problems with some of the early churches. According to tradition, he eventually went to Crete, where he served as bishop.

A thirty-two-year-old Protestant clergyman obtained a life reading and was told that his best line of work would be in the ministry or as a lawyer. Capable of showing much kindness and love to others, he was advised not to let his affection be misunderstood or taken to extremes by others. Extremely intelligent, he was reminded that he was the sum total of all he had applied in his sojourns in the earth.

In England during a period when there had been an attempt to separate church and state, he had been a blacksmith and a champion of freedom of speech and freedom of thought. Previous to that, he had lived in the Holy Land:

> Before that we find the entity in those days when the Master walked in the earth.
>
> The entity was a youth, and of Grecian parentage; coming under the ministry of Paul. And if there will be studied—alone—those epistles or letters written to the entity, as Titus, ye will find much of that admonition that at times becomes as living fires within the emotions of the inner self, and at

> others a rebellious force or not fully understood.
>
> The entity knew of, rather than being closely associated with the Master; yet those disciples or Apostles who came through that portion of the land—Andrew, James, Thaddeus, Thomas—all of those were not merely acquaintances but associates of the entity during that early portion of its experience.
>
> Yet those activities of the entity—especially in the churches of Asia Minor and the activities in Rome, when—in the latter portion of Paul's sojourn there—the acquaintance with Peter *and* Paul brought to the entity a *conviction* that will *ever* be that which causes it to proclaim, "There *can* be, there *is* only One church—even Jesus, the Christ!" 1842-1

During the time of Nehemiah and the rebuilding of the walls of the Holy City, [1842] had worked with mineral resources, creating binding materials for the stones that built the city walls. In Atlantis he had been a chemist, charged with assisting the Egyptians in making the lands about the Nile more productive for the raising of crops. In the present, he was reminded that it was that consciousness manifested in Jesus which he needed to emulate in his activities toward others. In the present, he was to assist individuals in understanding more about their relationship to the Creator. His reading predicted that throughout his life he would be asked to serve in the capacity of peacemaker.

Among the notations on file is a birthday greeting he sent to Edgar Cayce in 1939:

> What a delightful event a birthday must be for one who spends his life helping others, for with each passing year there must come increasingly the inevitable blessedness which is the lot of all who

> give rather than receive. May I take this simple but sincere means of wishing for you the happiest birthday you have ever had, and of expressing the hope that your fellow man may have occasion for many years to come to be thankful for your presence among us.

Over the next decade, [1842] corresponded with Hugh Lynn Cayce about his studies, his activities, and his hobbies. A letter in 1949 stated, "[I] am going to the seminary in August to begin work on my doctorate in theology. I intend to concentrate on the general field of 'Denominationalism.'" In 1954 he sent a change of address notice to A.R.E. and commented that he was going to be an associate professor of the Bible. No additional reports are on file.

Vashti
Esther 1-2
Case 1096

Vashti was King Ahasuerus's first queen. On the seventh day of an enormous banquet, the king, also known as Xerxes, summoned his wife and commanded that she display her beauty in front of his drunken guests. She refused to do so, so the enraged king deposed her as queen and found another woman, Esther, to be her replacement. (See also "Esther.") Because of Vashti's defiance, the king issued a proclamation declaring that a woman's husband was the ruler of every household.

A fifty-year-old divorced woman writer received confirmation in her life reading that one of her greatest talents was writing. Her most recent incarnation had been in Fort Dearborn, Chicago, as one who counseled and gave advice to the young, especially in terms of law and order. She had also been in the Netherlands, where she had provided others with a moral understanding of spiritual laws. In ancient Egypt she dedicated herself to service in the Temple Beautiful and eventually rose to a position of authority among her people. The lifetime having the greatest influence upon the present, however, was that of Vashti, queen to the king of Persia:

> Before that we find the entity was in the period when it was the *queen* of those peoples that held the peoples of the Promised Land in bondage; being then in the name Vashti, the queen of Ahasuerus.
>
> When another was chosen and the entity was to become demoted, there came the choice for those activities that held to the purposefulness of self—in keeping self in accord with those that were the moral laws of the entity, rather than enjoining with those things that might bring for the entity a position or pleasure for a season.
>
> From that experience, and those things that prompt the activity in which there are the contending influences with which the entity labored during that experience, there may be written by the entity the story that may become an *understanding* to many who are to meet—as the entity—the influences of that which is noble, beautiful, that is of the Creative Forces; yet degraded for a purpose that may make for exaltation of or the aggrandizement of a people, or of individuals, for a season.
>
> 1096-1

She was encouraged to use writing and to retell the story of Vashti from her perspective. Subsequent readings informed her that in spite of the hardships she had experienced as Vashti, she had gained an awareness that all souls (male and female) stand as one before the Creative Forces. Although only living at that time until the age of thirty-three, from then on she became a champion for women's rights.

According to the readings, she had been chosen as Queen Vashti at the age of sixteen. As the years passed, however, and no children were produced, many within the king's court made plans to depose her and find another queen so that continuation of the king's line would be insured. Vashti's refusal to appear at the banquet provided them with the means to fulfill their plans:

> With the refusal of Vashti (and this was only in the early portion of the twenties—in age—of Vashti), then there came the choosing of those that were to take the place of the queen.
>
> Hence we find, as would be termed in the present day, there was *proclaimed* a Beauty Pageant of the young women of the land.
>
> Why did Vashti fail to present herself at such a condition or period? It was not only because of the political influence of those that had been placed in power, and the pitting of the friendships as one against another, but because of the moral attitude owing to the religious tend as a follower of Zend.
>
> As to the experience of the entity following the rise of another to the place or position as queen, then, we find:
>
> The entity, after a period of separation, was *given* to a friend of the king as a companion. And this belittled or made for those innate influences that have been indicated that arise in the experience of the entity in its relationships in the present with friends, political affiliation and association, and the *doubts* that arise in the experience of the entity as to those that *have* dedicated themselves for an active service and in the *mind* of the entity (present) do not *sepa-*

> *rate* themselves from the activities of those that do otherwise. 1096-2

Gladys Davis noted that Mrs. [1096] was a very attractive woman and looked much younger than her years. Her first marriage had been to a well-known real estate developer whom she felt sure had been Ahasuerus (Xerxes), since the main cause of their divorce had been a big party in which he had insisted that she appear nude before his guests.

According to other reports, [1096] became very interested in the Cayce information on Persia. When she obtained a life reading for her second husband, she learned that he had been Haman, Ahasuerus's chief minister during her lifetime as Vashti. (See also "Haman.") In 1944, she informed A.R.E. that she was writing a book about the life of Vashti. She wrote to request a reading on the manuscript, but the appointment was eventually postponed because of Edgar Cayce's illness and later canceled because of his death. In 1945, a letter was written asking her about the status of her book on Vashti. Mrs. [1096] responded shortly thereafter:

> Upon reaching my home in the North last Friday I found your letter of the 24th of May and was indeed most pleased to hear from you. *Vashti* has been in my files for a long time; in fact, I have not even thought of her for years—but I do have such a good start on that book it seems a shame that my many activities keep from going on with it.
>
> You see, this winter I entered on a radio career—and I might add made a tremendous success, writing my own scripts and having a fifteen-minute broadcast each Sunday. I had to write and record twenty platters to leave until October when I will return . . . my sponsor . . . wish[es] to renew my con-

> tract for another six months in October. So you can well understand why *Vashti* reposes in my files . . . Thanking you for your very nice letter which has given me new heart to work on *Vashti* and trusting I may hear from you again in the very near future, I am, Sincerely [1096].

No detailed follow-up reports are on file.

Widow of Nain
Luke 7:11-17
Case 601

After entering Capernaum and healing the centurion's servant at a distance, Jesus and His disciples journeyed to the city of Nain. As they arrived, a great procession carried the body of a dead man out of the gates of the city. He was the only son of a woman who was also a widow. When Jesus saw her tears, He took compassion on her and told her, "Weep not." Jesus than approached the funeral bier, upon which they carried the dead man, touched it, and told the young man to arise. The young man sat up and spoke to his mother, and all the people became amazed and fearful, marveling to see the demonstration of the power that Jesus possessed.

During the course of her life reading, a forty-eight-year-old housewife was told that she had lived two past lives that were noted in Scripture. One was as Sheluenmehei, a daughter to King David (see also "Sheluenmehei"); the other was as the widow of Nain:

> Before that we find (among those that influence in the present) the entity was during those periods when there were the activities in what is now known as the Promised Land, during those periods when the Christ—or Jesus—walked in the earth.

The entity then was among those peoples that were aided by the ministry of this teacher, this master, during that sojourn; of those peoples to whom the entity received back alive the son—as they walked from Nain at those periods of His ministry there.

Then in the name Deul, much of turmoil and strife came into the entity's experience; yet in the soul and mental forces of the entity much was gained during that sojourn. There was the embracing of those activities, yet following very closely in what—in its own activities—may be called the very orthodox in the presenting of self to the peoples for the service during that activity; yet being enjoined to those that were of a different faith brought much of turmoil in the mental and in the soul forces, though developments were gained by the entity in and during that sojourn in that land. For much of peoples' minds, much of peoples' activities, came under the vision and the experience of the entity during that particular sojourn; making for an experience wherein there has been oft in the experience of the entity—even during the present—those things pertaining to the activities seen and viewed by the entity during that period, that have brought into the experience much that has been the *saving* influence—it may be said—as to its *belief,* as to its activity in relationship to those things pertaining to what is termed religious thought. Not, then, as an orthodox individual nor a fundamentalist, but rather as one that has seen a vision, an experience, and has *not* let it pass without those things that have added to the greatness of the abilities to which the entity may give itself to others during this sojourn. 601-2

From her experience as the widow of Nain, she was excellent at ministering to others and in helping people to create a helpful home environment.

Extremely interested in the Cayce work for several years, [601] obtained readings for herself and for other family members. She died of cancer in 1938.

Zebedee

Matthew 4:18-22, 10:1-4, 20:20-28, 26:36-44, 27:55-56; Mark 1:16-20, 3:14-19, 10:35-45; Luke 5:1-11; John 21:1-14
Case 420

Zebedee was a fisherman on the Sea of Galilee and the father of James and John, two of Jesus' apostles. A successful businessman, he had hired servants and apparently helped finance some of the needs of Jesus and His followers.

In 1942, a sixty-two-year-old bill collector who was very active in his Episcopal church learned that the lifetime that was having the greatest influence on his present experience was one in Palestine:

> For, in the period when the Master walked in the house, in that home from whom there were the selecting of the two outstanding disciples in that group, the entity was then the father of James and John—and in the name Zebedee.[8]
>
> The entity then was given to the obtaining and leasing of privileges to others, and was engaged—as were the sons—in the fleets, or fishing; though

[8]A file notation from 1942 states that a twenty-year-old Catholic college student, [1089], obtained a life reading and was also told that his name had been Zebedee; however, from the reading itself Gladys Davis surmised that [1089] had actually been the *father* of Zebedee and, therefore, the grandfather of James and John.

these were only a small part of the entity's activities itself.

Coming under those influences, at first the entity was averse to the interest shown by James and John. Then, with the better acquaintance, the entity grew into that attitude which is exhibited in the present—a greater advocate of the "all out" administration of self and of self's abilities, and of self's physical, mental and material abilities, for the welfare of those in spiritual truth.

As was manifested or maintained by the entity in that experience, as maintained and growing in the present—a stickler for a set rule of formality, yet that also of the perfect—or more perfect—understanding of the true meaning of those abilities for one to be tolerant with others.

This is thy greater virtue, then, in the present. That needed for greater manifestation is also akin—patience. In these the entity grows. Keep that growth. 420-6

Additional past lives included one as a town clerk during the colonial period, where he had acquired his interest in keeping and maintaining records. In Persia, he had been involved in using gold, minerals, and precious metals as methods of foreign exchange. In ancient Egypt, he had been one of those charged with keeping law and order.

In the present, he was told that his best activities were in any field that enabled him to utilize his innate creativity, making conveniences and inventions for the home. He was encouraged to become more patient in his attitude toward others. His reading also acknowledged that he would have made a good politician, utilizing some of the skills he had acquired as a town clerk. The advice given to him was to work in "any field of service where ye may serve thy fellow man, in dealing out justice to all . . . And in those things of spiritual nature, give them that insight thou obtained when ye mended nets and listened to His second sermon by the sea."

Prior to obtaining his own life reading, Mr. [420] commented on the effectiveness of the physical readings he had obtained for himself and his family, including a son:

> This boy was cured, when medical aid failed. My wife, [379], mother-in-law, and myself have been most wonderfully helped. One of the outstanding qualities of a reading is its individuality. The diagnosis of the patient is perfect, and if the suggestions are followed they are sure to bring results.

In 1947, [420] suffered a stroke; however, after he used some of the treatments that had been recommended in the readings for others, his wife reported that her husband seemed perfectly normal and well. Although he was weak, he was not paralyzed at all. A notation from 1949 states that he had retired from his job, but was very active with his hobby of woodworking in his shop at home.

The final file report is from June 1957: Mr. [420] died after being bedridden for about a year.

Zuekido
I Chronicles 3:19
Case 991

Zerubbabel was the first individual to lead a group of Israelites back to Jerusalem from their exile in Babylon. A governor of Jerusalem, he directed the resumption of worship, the rebuilding of the altar, and the foundation construction for the new temple. Among Zerubbabel's children, according to Edgar Cayce, was a son named Zuekido, who had returned with his father to Jerusalem to help rebuild the city; he is not mentioned by name in the Bible.

In 1935, a thirty-nine-year-old rabbi learned that his past incarnations were having opposing influences on his present life. For that reason, he would often be at a crossroads in life, making decisions that would lead him in one direction or another. Essentially, those influences would either move him in the way of serving God or in the direction of satisfying his own physical desires, as he had done in "the fleshpots of Egypt."

His most recent incarnation had been as a Frenchman trading furs in the United States in the areas around New York, Pennsylvania, Michigan, and Illinois. As a Catholic in that incarnation, he had gained an innate understanding of true Christian virtue rather than simply theology. Prior to that, he had been in the Holy Land:

> Before that we find the entity was in that period when there was the return of the children of promise from captivity to the rebuilding of the walls of the city, to the rebuilding of the temple itself.
>
> Then as Zuekido, the son of Zerubbabel, the entity labored at the rebuilding; and was set as one of the sons who kept and gathered the tax that was to assist in the reestablishing of the temple service.
>
> The entity then, being overzealous as to those activities, was rebuked not only by those under Nehemiah but those in the second return—as Ezra.
>
> Hence those things recorded as of Nehemiah's and Ezra's writings have in the entity a feeling of insecurity, insincerity; for the rebuke was deep to the entity. For had not the entity felt that those who were able to pay *should pay* for those who were *unable* to pay?
>
> Hence the *innate* feelings were higher even than the priesthood; and the entity was banished, be-

> coming among those that—as it were—followed from afar. Yet the entity aided mightily with its bodily strength in building up the city, in building up the walls roundabout. 991-1

From that incarnation, in spite of his early zealousness, he had come to understand "that God loveth mercy and justice rather than ritual or might . . . "

During a lifetime in Persia, he had been a scribe and a teacher of Zoroastrianism. He had also been in ancient Egypt, serving as a diplomat and as one involved in healing. At the same time, however, he had apparently satisfied his physical appetites.

In the present, he possessed abilities as a teacher, a writer, and a lecturer and was told that he could coordinate the teachings of the East and the West. His reading advised him: "Correlate not the differences, but where all religions meet—*there is one God!* 'Know, O Israel, the Lord thy God is *one!*'"

When he asked about the advisability of traveling to Palestine, his reading told him not to go but rather to remain in service as a rabbi, a teacher, and a minister in Chicago, Connecticut, Detroit, or Cleveland. Again, he was encouraged to write books. When he asked why he was interested in both Christianity and Judaism, the reply came: "Hast thou not tried both? Hast thou not found that the *essence,* the truth, the *real* truth is *one?*"

A mutual friend later reported that [991] was so thrilled about his reading that he could hardly talk about it. Shortly thereafter, Rabbi [991] wrote Edgar Cayce regarding his own confusion about what he should do and the fact that "black forces" were attacking him constantly. The mutual friend heard in September 1935 that [991] had decided to go to Palestine, where he planned to sell refrigerators. By 1939, however, he had returned to New York.

The last file entry is from 1943, when it was reported that he was still struggling with his attempts to live a spiritual life. At the time he was terribly confused and admitted to being unfaithful to his wife and having a mistress who was seven months' pregnant.

Afterword

From the case history files of the Edgar Cayce readings it becomes evident that reincarnation emphasizes a continuity of existence. Life does not begin at physical birth and then end some seven to ten decades later. Instead, it is a continuous process. Although physical life may appear to be limited by a finite number of years, a soul's individuality is an ongoing expression in which each individual is the sum total of all she or he has ever been.

Truly, life is a process of personal growth and evolution whereby choices and activities in the past help to create the framework for potentials and possibilities in the present. In turn, choices in the present begin to form an array of probable futures. At the soul level, talents and abilities as well as desires and shortcomings become a part of personal awareness where they may be cultivated and worked with or transformed and worked through. From the perspective of the Edgar Cayce material, this process of soul growth will eventually enable all individuals to conform to an innate pattern of spirituality and possess an awareness of their true relationship with God and the rest of creation. The success of the soul is inevitable; it is simply a matter of time.

Of the thousands of names mentioned in the past-life readings of Edgar Cayce, approximately seventy individuals were told that they had been a biblical character from the annals of history. However, rather than emphasizing the importance of these particular lifetimes, the readings suggested that these physical expressions were no more or no less important than the soul histories of any other individual. As far as Cayce was concerned, one's spiritual value was not determined by who he or she had been in the past but how the individual applied what she or he knew to do in the present. To be sure, each lifetime is an important and purposeful experience, but reincarnation is the great leveler of humankind. Throughout the case histories of the Cayce files, it appears as though most souls have both "gained and lost" in their passage through time and space.

The reality of this growth and retrogression is clearly evident in many of the stories contained in the Bible, for within its pages one can find innumerable patterns of human experience and behavior. Although extremely informative within themselves, when these individual life stories are also viewed within the framework of reincarnation—enabling one to see what came before as well as the result thereafter—the continuity of the soul becomes more than simply a philosophical notion. In fact, by exploring the soul histories of others there is much one might learn about the nature of one's own.

A.R.E. Press

The A.R.E. Press publishes quality books, videos, and audiotapes meant to improve the quality of our readers' lives—personally, professionally, and spiritually. We hope our products support your endeavors to realize your career potential, to enhance your relationships, to improve your health, and to encourage you to make the changes necessary to live a loving, joyful, and fulfilling life.

For more information or to receive a free catalog, call:

1-800-723-1112

Or write:

A.R.E. Press
215 67th Street
Virginia Beach, VA 23451-2061